DERAL J. JOHNSON

Choral Techniques: Beyond the Basics

Practical suggestions for choral conductors of school groups and community and church choirs.

kjos NEIL A. KJOS MUSIC COMPANY • Publisher

ISBN 0-8497-4184-X

CONTENTS

Preface

This handbook has been written in response to, and at the request of, those who have suffered emotional trauma while taking choral technique classes under my tutelage. Former students requesting that such a compilation of notes, ideas, and wild solutions given in class be put in print surely know the price to be paid in memories of our times together. I decided to go ahead, no matter the consequences. The classroom demonstrations of the various topics are, unfortunately omitted from this handbook.

This is not a book for beginners. It is for those who already possess an elementary knowledge of conducting and wish to upgrade their skills.

Many of the ideas presented pertain to the inner workings of the body and mind. Since each body is different, suggestions directed toward a certain part of the anatomy will induce a different feeling from one individual to the next. My only hope is to direct the conductor toward solutions for frustrating choral problems.

I wish to express my appreciation to Louis Dierks who many years ago started me thinking about individual voice quality and its importance when putting together a choral ensemble.

Nancy Telfer, when visiting us in Texas, asked to see the chapters I had put together in rough form and immediately placed me on probation until the finished product came to fruition! She, at that time, took the responsibility for contributing detailed and very helpful suggestions which were much appreciated. Dr. Victoria Meredith indicated early on that she would like to look through the manuscript, and once again I received wonderful ideas from an excellent conductor and rehearsal artist. Many thanks to both of you!

My wife, Marie, who has been helpful throughout my career, contributed extensively to the clarification of concepts throughout the course of this undertaking. You will note that she has included (with daughter Marsha's assistance) a very important chapter on choral accompanying. She was also the computer expert and for too many days a slave of that keyboard. What a congenial co-worker she is; it has been my privilege to experience her helpfulness since 1950.

Deral Johnson

About the Author

Deral Johnson is Professor Emeritus at the University of Western Ontario where he was Director of Choral Activities for 23 years. During his tenure at Western, the number of choirs grew from one to five and the choral techniques courses developed from one course to four courses in seven sections. The UWO Faculty of Music Singers (a student choir), which Johnson conducted, was privileged to perform twice for national ACDA conventions (Kansas City and New Orleans). This choir won several awards including two first-place awards in the 1986 CBC radio competitions and a first place in the 1987 Let the People Sing International Choral Competition.

Johnson was the recipient of the 1992 National Choral Award for Outstanding Service in Choral Education presented by the Association of Canadian Choral Conductors. In 1996 he received the Silver Anniversary Award for Distinguished Service to Choral Music in Ontario, given by the Ontario Choral Federation.

Over the years Professor Johnson has been active as adjudicator and clinician in the U.S. and Canada. He has conducted all-province choirs, community choral groups, and church choirs.

Johnson's career began as a teacher in elementary and secondary schools in Kansas and Texas. He then taught vocal and choral music at Colorado University and Hastings College. He earned degrees from Sterling College and Northern Colorado University, and did advanced graduate studies at the University of Colorado.

CHAPTER

I

THE CHORAL DISCIPLINE—A DISTINCTIVE ARTISTIC ENDEAVOR

Music is an uniquely rewarding discipline. The successful performer portrays an aesthetic awareness that touches basic emotions within both performer and listener. The achievement of this aesthetic experience, however, depends on the discipline of the performer and understanding the chosen instrument.

The choral conductor, in addition to understanding the unique properties of the individual voice, must be able to combine a group of vocal instruments to produce an aesthetically and emotionally pleasing performance ensemble. Success in this endeavor requires the development of a personal philosophy and sense of discipline.

It is my purpose in this handbook to help this development by identifying pitfalls that many choral conductors encounter and by suggesting practical approaches to choral organization, rehearsal procedures, and the development of quality ensemble tone production. The following are just a few that will be expanded upon in succeeding chapters.

A Unique Instrument

One concern of the conductor is an understanding of the singer-musician's instrument and its unique characteristics and requirements. The vocalist possesses an instrument that is inside the physical body and is connected both directly and indirectly to the muscular and nervous systems. The vocal performer, therefore, must develop and nurture an instrument that cannot be seen, felt, or touched. As they are not usually natural and instinctive, sensations relating to proper tonal placement need to be discovered and developed. Muscles involved in tone production should be exercised and systematically trained. It is necessary, also, for both singer and conductor to understand the connection between emotional health and the basic tone-producing instrument.

The requirements of this unique instrument often cause the vocal performer to become preoccupied with his or her instrument to the exclusion of other fundamentals of musical discipline that are of equal, if not greater, importance. The serious vocalist, consequently, is often frustrated in the attempt to develop a balance between honoring the integrity of the music and giving due attention to the physical feelings of correct production. Understanding of both of these elements is necessary, however, for the development of a performer capable of being part of a satisfying choral experience.

Developing the Instrument

The choral conductor is blessed if voice teachers possessing similar vocal philosophies are instructing each member of the choral ensemble. The majority of conductors in the business cannot, however, rely on such good fortune. Conductors must, therefore, become acquainted with the physical structure of the voice and with well-developed ideas on vocal improvements. When listening to a choir, one quickly notices the dramatic differences in voice qualities, the uniqueness of each instrument, and the highly individualized responses given by the ensemble sections (soprano, alto, tenor, bass).

It is assumed that the reader has studied voice either privately or within the context of a choir. A dramatic first step, then, for the choral\vocal expert is to expand upon the knowledge of vocal challenges and solutions beyond the techniques acquired during individual voice training. The conductor must be aware that the difficulties encountered in his or her own singing development will often be different from those experienced by individuals in the choral organization. New problems will be discovered and, therefore, new solutions must be researched through the study of books or through consultation with singing professionals.

An understanding of this wide range of voice problems and solutions (including plausible vocal remedies suggested in several of the excellent contemporary books on the subject) is a requirement for the conductor. This knowledge will be of assistance in making effective vocal evaluation and improvement within a choral organization.

Choral Sounds

Conductors should not allow themselves to be forced into a narrowness that reduces the number of options available for producing a good choral sound. Though they should not be ignored, influences from other choral conductors and the so-called academic elite who favor compartmentalization of styles and interpretative approaches should not entirely restrict the conductor's creative choices.

In addition, conductors may be pressured to reflect a specialization (including type of vocal production) in Renaissance, Baroque, Classic, Romantic, Contemporary, Late Contemporary, Pop Culture, or whatever is in vogue. The successful conductor must be brave enough to follow a middle ground and be thoughtful and flexible in his or her approaches to choral performance.

Discipline and Organization

A most irksome, but necessary, part of the professional life of a choral conductor is instilling discipline and organization into each singer/performer of the ensemble. The frequently used statement that a rehearsal or performance is 98% perspiration and 2% inspiration is correct.

Media influences and peer pressures on individuals can interfere with the conductor's ability to convince ensemble members of the need for honest self-criticism and personal discipline. Yet, if the artist who is dedicated to high performance standards cannot persuade the ensemble to be disciplined and aware, a vital portion of individual musical development and appreciation will be lost.

How and when the conductor instills self-discipline and musical awareness in the ensemble is difficult to determine. The conductor eventually learns to rely on intuition and common sense to provide guidance as to when the ensemble is in need of a reprimand, a pat on the back, a moment of reflection, or a time to just laugh.

The use of intuition and common sense, however, does not necessarily suggest the use of no plan at all. The conductor's strategy for achieving performance goals should be thought out before the rehearsal, and applied in a direct, positive manner. The conductor/disciplinarian, of course, should be a person who possesses solid self-discipline (an idea which may be a frightening notion for some directors).

Choral Music Repertoire

No matter how busy the ensemble conductor, time should be set aside for finding music literature that is intellectually and technically stimulating, and that will provide members of the group with a sense of accomplishment. This feeling of achievement will contribute uniquely to the vitality of the ensemble.

Choral conductors often "give in" when approached with the request to perform shallow, easy materials that ensemble members claim to like, rather than presenting challenging materials which singers will soon come to appreciate. An essential realization is that individual technical improvement in performance will only take place when the work ethic is the accepted norm and challenges are met with vigor.

Enthusiasm in performance is a result of rehearsals in which the conductor points out the specific musical ideas and then provides technical solutions. If the chosen literature encourages revealing analysis and the approach to such revelation is exciting, an ensemble will respond with enthusiasm and vitality.

Research and Performance

Because of the great number of fine music historians, the prolific output of contemporary musicologists, and the academic background of many of our prominent choral leaders today, we can be somewhat frustrated by the different and varied ideas literally thrown at us from all directions by so many authorities in books and in workshops. Each expert rightfully considers his or her researched concepts to be the correct performance practice, with its choral tone implications. Whom do we trust and how do we find a way through the maze of ideas and solutions concerning choral music performance?

The key word is "performance." If the carefully researched concept produces a dull and uninteresting performance, then one must carefully weigh the merits of such an approach. Some ideas concerning "correct" ensemble performance can stimulate little interest and less excitement.

A primary task for the choral conductor is to adopt degrees of compromise between musicological and performance requirements. An effort must be made to maintain both the musical integrity of the composition and the ability of the literature to communicate to the choir member and to the listener. Unfortunately, the easiest way out of the dilemma is to do as one has been taught without giving thought to the performance consequences.

How fortunate we are to have the careful research by many knowledgeable experts. Our concern as choral experts is to develop the wisdom that enables us to find solutions which will accommodate musicological requirements and still provide stimulation and interest among ensemble members, healthy vocal production, and aesthetically satisfying performances.

Techniques and Communication

To have a choir know exactly what is expected of them through the use of the conductor's hands rather than the mouth is a beautiful experience for both ensemble and conductor. In order to efficiently accomplish her or his goals, the conductor must develop conducting habits which are communicative, clear, and concise.

Choral conducting is an art, and as in any artistic endeavor, some questions will remain unanswered. The challenge and work involved in attempting to find answers, however, is most rewarding. Perhaps the following chapters will be of assistance in finding solutions to some of the problems touched on in this first chapter.

CHAPTER

THE EARS

In this chapter, matters pertaining to the training of the conductor's ears, and sensitizing the ears of the ensemble will be considered. The conductor definitely has the advantage when one thinks of the physical placement of the ears. The performing vocalist, on the other hand, may very well think it's nature's cruel joke to have ears on the sides. (One might wonder how attractive a human being would be if the ears were positioned in locations useful to the performer.)

The Conductor
The conductor of an ensemble listens to the group of performers in the same manner as listening to fine stereo speakers. Problems of stereo balance or of amplifier distortion are perceived quickly when one has discriminating hearing capabilities.

When a conductor is in front of a choral ensemble, general problems of balance and intonation can be located just as easily. The real challenge comes when a conductor wishes to know which individual is spoiling the corporate sectional tone or who is bringing the pitch down in a particular section. Most individuals are not blessed with sharp, directional hearing; they must develop this skill.

Exercise 1: Directional hearing is not only learned in front of an ensemble but may be nurtured outside the rehearsal room. Generally, in a cafeteria or in a crowded area many conversations are taking place (from serious to idiotic to intimate). When a conductor is in the midst of such a cacophony of sound and is free to do so, a conscious effort to aim the hearing process toward a conversation across the crowded room (might make a title for a song) is a most rewarding ear-training exercise. At times, the experience might be too enriching if the conversation is of a "restricted" category, but the ear trainee does have the option of directing attention to another part of the hall for interesting tidbits of consumable information.

Exercise 2: Another exercise recommended for the individual who wishes to train a more discriminating directional ear is to listen for individual instruments or voices when enjoying a live performance of an ensemble. This exercise, at times, takes away from the total pleasure of ensemble listening, but it does offer a relaxed approach to ear training.

Complete dedication to directional hearing can, however, cause the conductor some confusion. If the conductor believes that the choir must be balanced as far as sections are concerned and that a homogenous sound of voices is desirable, then much of the time must be spent listening to the ensemble for overall balance and blend. (See Chapter VI for more information on blend.) A conductor, therefore, will probably always be troubled with the necessity of making quick changes from directional hearing duties to wide spectrum hearing duties.

The Singer
The ensemble member, on the other hand, has a totally different problem when it comes to the discipline of listening. As previously mentioned, the ears of the human being are not positioned well for the singer to hear her or his own tonal and pitch contribution, nor are the ears placed efficiently for correctional balance with other voices. For the singers' ears to be most effective they should probably be extendible, large, directionally controllable and completely sensitive to all changes in pitch and power. Obviously, the singer must learn to do the best possible with reality.

The conductor needs to understand the practical facts concerning an ensemble member's inability to hear what the conductor is hearing. For the singer to hear her or his own voice accurately it is necessary to place both hands in front of the face and adjust this "sounding board" so it reflects the voice to both ears. A simple cupping of a hand over one ear gives little indication of pitch or true quality of tone. In fact, such a procedure will many times provide inaccurate information, for the sound has to bounce off someone or something to return to the cupped single ear. Such an acoustical bounce is rarely accurate.

Most of us do not have ears with equal decibel range or clarity of sound. When each singer is standing next to other singers, each ear might well register a slight variation in tuning and general sound. The ensemble member, therefore, must adjust to what his or her hearing mechanism is really indicating (sounds interpreted by the brain as a result of learned responses) and to put very little trust in the basic inner ear. It is not as much a matter of learning to listen carefully as it is of learning to automatically adjust the hearing mechanism for accuracy in tuning, volume, and clarity with little regard for extraneous influences.

Over the years I have found that the quickest way for singers to experience proper adjustment of general hearing skills is to indiscriminately mix the voices in rehearsal and ask for a different mix in succeeding rehearsals. For some reason mixing the voices creates an immediate necessity to strengthen the hearing abilities. A simple cautionary statement ("listen to each other") just won't accomplish this goal. Instructions to the ensemble member should aim toward teaching the singer to be as flexible as possible. The singer must be informed of incorrect tuning or troublesome volume, but she or he should then try to evaluate the situation and use inherent good sense and learned responses to consciously correct the problem at that point and as it arises in the future. The cultivation of self-discipline is never out of style.

Unfortunately, some singers may be handicapped by the fact that so many have lost approximately 10 to 20% of their hearing by being exposed to high decibel music and a noise-polluted society. This fact presents quite a challenge to those who are training choirs. The conductor must be more emphatic when asking for critical listening from the ensemble members, but sensitive to each individual's hearing capabilities.

CHAPTER
III

CONDUCTING TECHNIQUES

The gestures used when conducting an ensemble will likely be more effective if one concentrates on making the patterns simple and straightforward. Overly athletic instructions are counterproductive. It takes too much time for an ensemble to become accustomed to corkscrew gyrations, flailing and flapping of the hand, and guessing where the beat is.

Often, much of the communication between choir and conductor is verbal and little attention is paid to the conductor's hand instructions. The rehearsal will be much more efficient if the hands indicate the ideas to be explored without the mouth getting in the way. It is sometimes difficult for those of us in the information business to realize that the eyes often pick up more information than the ears. This means, then, that we must have the moves of an actor and/or ballet dancer and the same amount of control and precision.

Remember that there is an imaginary horizontal line below which the beat should not go. This line should be high enough to be seen by all performers. When the hand touches the line a point of contact (beat point) is established. The space between these points of contact can be used constructively in various ways. See Illustration 1.

Illustration 1

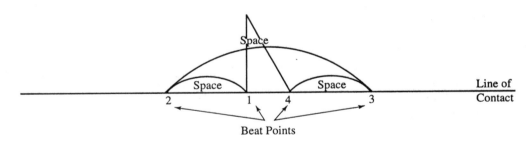

Beat Points

Much of the character of the composition can be communicated to the choir if one trains the conducting hand to approach the space between beats in a manner designed to set the desired musical style. A widely rounded line portrays richness and beauty, whereas a straight line can indicate a straightforward, perhaps martial, effect, and a bounce from beat to line might set the ensemble to thinking of a light-hearted, almost "frisky," approach to the music. If these hand indications are enhanced by similar facial expressions, verbal explanations can be shortened and one can save valuable rehearsal time.

Whether conducting with a baton or without, the position of the conducting hand has much influence over the response and well-being of the ensemble. The hand should give the exact beat without physical tension. A tense hand with stiff fingers protruding can cause tension and stridency in the voices of a choir with resulting sharpness in pitch. Conversely, a sloppy, limp hand tends to produce imprecision and a flat pitch.

As a conductor it is often necessary to battle normal inclinations in order to present constructive musical communication. For example, the interpretation of a beautiful, smooth, soft, slow passage becomes more interesting with the use of a motionless wrist. A fast and rhythmical passage takes on more "flash" if the wrist is moving. For me, these techniques bring feelings opposite to what seems normal, and objective effort must be made to use effective movements.

The left hand (or right if the left hand is the main communicating hand) can be of great help in producing and enhancing drama, or it can be merely a pathetic appendage to the body. The left hand must be trained to use movements completely detached from those of the right-hand. Its main duty is to contribute to the interpretation of the composition.

One must feel as though the left hand belongs to a ballet dancer or a mime. Drama, rather than the beat, is expressed through the left hand. Any exercise which will declare independence for the left arm and hand is useful and necessary. For example, while beating a series of patterns with your right hand, with your left hand pick up a book, comb your hair, produce dramatic gestures, or devise your own creative techniques.

Most conductors tend to fall into rather sloppy habits during their careers. A review should be made yearly concerning beat pattern, beat clarity, and the ability of the beat pattern to indicate musical style and ideas. Self-evaluation through videotaped rehearsals and performances, as well as honest dialogue with respected colleagues can prove useful in this regard. The following checklist may be helpful.

1. Is the area between beat points even rather than uneven and erratic, and the line of contact points horizontal?
2. Am I using a beat that is clear in all situations?
3. Is the beat pattern centered with my body?
4. Do I avoid gesturing with a sloppy wrist indicating several beat points for each beat.
5. Is the elbow either too far out or too close to the body (each position tends to create tension)?
6. Am I dictating the mood of the composition by
   a) using a bouncing beat for a rhythmical, sprightly composition?
   b) directing with straight lines between beats for a stately approach to the music?
   c) using lines between the beats that are rounded for long, lovely musical thoughts?
   d) using the left hand to enhance the drama and not as a mirror image of the right hand?
   e) avoiding the use of a fist or very stiff hand when conducting?
7. Is my pattern flexible enough to allow large gestures for loud passages and small gestures for soft?

One of the better books for help in renewing beat pattern direction is *Conducting Technique For Beginners And Professionals* by Brock McElheran (Oxford University Press, 1966). It takes only a short time to read, but the specific help given is valuable to both experienced and inexperienced conductors.

CHAPTER
IV

EFFICIENT USE OF THE VOICE
(with emphasis on vowels and consonants)

So much has been written about the importance of correct vowel formation and exact consonant articulation that it almost appears unnecessary to add to the impressive material available. Suffice it to say that without proper vowel placement the tone will be unpleasant, the sound will not carry, the pitch may be uncertain, and muscular tensions may develop which could be damaging to the voice. Without attention to consonants, the words will not be understood and tone production will tend to move toward the back of the mouth and hinder total vocal efficiency.

The purpose of this chapter is to indicate how this information relates to voices working together as a group. The individual in the group must physically sense correct vowel production and exact consonant weight. Suggestions placed before an ensemble must promote this response from each singer.

It has been observed that choral directors often, from the first day of rehearsal, demand "beautiful sounds" from a choir without giving needed technical training. If the group consists entirely of trained voices, the demand from the conductor for "beautiful sounds" may be practical, although specific descriptive terminology might be more helpful (i.e., "dark," "bright," etc.). Most choirs, however, include a number of untrained singers, and a teaching approach is needed.

Just as instrumental teachers do not expect immediate, mature tones from amateur organizations, a choir director should not expect unified sounds at the first rehearsals. The conductor should be prepared to begin teaching the techniques which will allow each chorister to develop flexibility and improve his or her own sound.

VOWELS

Effective vowel placement is the basis for a beautiful tone-carrying quality. Most amateur vocalists must experience new sensations relative to the physical placement of the vowel. Individual experimentation does not immediately create ensemble tonal beauty, but it does set the stage for basic improvement which leads to the desired ensemble sound.

One necessity of voice training is an understanding and development of basic vibrating mediums which sets into motion all the acoustical resonators needed to produce tone. The "ee" [i] and "ay" [e] sounds are the only vowels which tend to activate this primary sound vibration (see William Vennard's *Singing, the Mechanism and the Technic*, Carl Fischer, Inc., 1967). Although these vowels have a tendency to seem most unpleasant to the singer and provide a less than satisfying experience for the conductor, promotion of the physical attention needed for basic sound vibration (through the use of these two vowel sounds) appears to be the quickest way toward vowel efficiency.

A pucker of the lips will help the "ee" and "ay" vowels to comfortably develop a controlled, pleasant, tone quality. The "ah" [a] and "oh" [o] vowels are quickly and efficiently fused into this constant ring of sound through exercises that keep all physical feelings of vowel production toward the front of the mouth. (Exercises that alternate "ee" or "ay" with "ah" or "oh" while allowing little change in the position of the mouth will promote a physical feeling of steady ringing sound. Exercises such as "ee ah ee ah ee ah" used in arpeggiated sequence, or "ay ee ah ee oh ay ah ee oh ee" are most productive.)

After tone placement has become secure as a result of the above exercises, mouth position can be somewhat adjusted. "Smile" for the "oh" and "ah" vowels and "pucker" for the "ee" and "ay" vowels (with an open and relaxed mouth) is not a bad creed for the singer to live by if used in moderation. As an extra benefit, faulty pitch seems to be corrected when the lips are used in a way that adds body rather than brightness to vowel coloring. It is desirable for the chorister to understand that the mouth is open and relaxed and that it is not to be placed in contorted positions. The less the mouth moves the more even the color of the sound and the more flexible the singer.

Some ensemble participants may not be thrilled with the new physical feeling of tone production—the "ee's" may feel too dull and the "oh's" too light and airy. With time, these physical feelings will become natural and even pleasant if developed diligently. The only ensemble members who have no need for such exercises are those who have natural open resonance or those who are already well-trained vocally.

The Tongue and Vowel Coloration

The tongue seems to be the forgotten part of our anatomy when it comes to pure vowel coloration. It is more than a physical entity to be positioned at the bottom of the mouth where it remains inactive.

The "ih" [I], "eh" [ɛ], and "uh" [ə] vowels are frequently mispronounced and interchanged. Their difference lies in the position of the tongue, making the tongue of practical importance in producing pure vowel coloring. Vowels need to be individualistic in nature if diction in any language is to be understandable. The word "bitter," for example, can turn very quickly into "better" if the "ih" sound is not well defined.

The back of the tongue controls the flow of each vowel sound. The conductor must guide the singer's choice of tongue position by indicating when the correct sound is being produced. An exercise to assist in this development is to have the choir members go through the vowels ee, ih, eh, uh, with the only physical movement being that of the back of the tongue.

If ensemble members can be directed to keep the tip of the tongue in the area of the bottom teeth or gum ridge, the large portion of the tongue can be freed to develop the sound positioning needed for vowel placement. A rather immediate result of such tongue control is a more relaxed mouth and better tuning.

If the sounds of the "ah" and "oh" are not directed to the front of the mouth a flat pitch is inevitable. Conversely, by directing the "ee" vowel through too small a channel, a sharp pitch can be expected.

We must always have relaxation in mind when singing. The tongue can be the root of many severe problems if the concept of muscular relaxation is not emphasized. For example:

1. A fast vibrato is often the result of too much tension at the base or back of the tongue.
2. Sharpness in pitch can be caused by tension in the forward portion of the tongue.
3. Metallic sounds are almost always the result of a tense tongue.
4. Improper budgeting of breath sometimes is caused by tensions at the tongue base.

Vocal problems often have to be solved by working indirectly. If the offending area is too frequently mentioned, most singers, particularly amateurs, will be drawn to a mental picture that subconsciously creates tension in that area.

One of the challenges for the choral teacher is in finding ways to train the tongue to help vocal production without adding anxiety caused by frequently mentioning its important role. To overcome tongue tension and misplacement, a rather silly diet of exercises may range from requiring the ensemble to babble completely unintelligible strings of words (using all the "l's" possible) to drawing a finger down the middle of the tongue (clean finger, of course).

Hearing Correct Vowel Sounds.

While the ensemble singer is still experimenting with the vocal instrument, both the conductor and the performer must begin a fine-tuning of the ear. The conductor acts as the outside ears for the ensemble member and the ensemble member sets the physical mechanisms into motion to program the connection between correct vowel production and the hearing of such correctness from inside the body.

Since the typical ensemble member is not able to hear his own voice properly, it is not possible to discriminate between the poorly produced vowel and the open, well-placed vowel. The conductor of a choral ensemble must develop the ability to hear the best of vowel qualities produced by the ensemble member and then indicate to the singer the type of sound being projected.

In all probability the individual speaking habits of ensemble members will not be dramatically changed. Singing diction habits, however, will develop a clarity and smoothness which, while producing pleasant tone, will promote easy understanding of text.

Experimentation by the singers, both in the ensemble and individually outside the group, is the key to successfully solving the mysteries of proper vowel production.

CONSONANTS

Consonants give meaning and understanding to words. When used in an efficient, relaxed manner, consonants should help the voice stabilize sound production based on good vowel construction.

Different consonants require different amounts of attention during rehearsal. For example:

1. Consonants which require the most work from the ensemble member are those which promote little sound. The "*f*" and "*p*," for example, have no tone involvement and, therefore, must be given high priority during rehearsal.
2. Consonants which have vibrations of both lips and teeth, such as "v," "b," and "th" (as in these), should be given second priority for special rehearsal work.
3. "D's" and "t's" are low in priority and should require little attention during rehearsal.
4. The consonant "s" is an unpleasant sound which should usually have its power diminished.
5. The "k" and "g" consonants can detrimentally direct the flow of tone into the throat if not constantly projected as far forward as possible.
6. The semi-consonants "l" and "r" are in a category of their own, for they are quite ugly when sung from the back of the mouth as a vowel rather than a consonant. Both should be physically produced at the front of the mouth by the upper teeth and tongue. To hold either of these semi-consonants as a continuing tone will restrict the tone and produce a flatness of pitch as well as a less than satisfactory sound.

An effort should be made to place all consonants as far forward in the mouth as possible. This will help to project good tonal quality as well as make the word more easily understood.

Clear, useful information concerning consonant structure can be found in *Singing, the Mechanism and the Technic* by William Vennard (Carl Fischer, 1967).

CHAPTER

V

VOICE INDIVIDUALITIES AND SECTIONAL PERSONALITIES OF CHORAL ENSEMBLES

Two of the goals of the choral conductor are the development of good blend and accurate intonation within the ensemble. Blend and intonation interact upon each other in such a way that the improvement of one often strengthens the other.

In order to achieve these two goals it is necessary to be aware of and to deal with (1) the vocal qualities of the individual singer and (2) the personalities of each section of the choir. The purpose of this chapter is to isolate the inherent problems in dealing with blend and intonation and offer some practical suggestions and solutions.

VOICE INDIVIDUALITIES

One of the first facts discovered when working with a choral ensemble is that there are many differences in both the individual vocal qualities of the singers and in the sound-carrying power of their voices. The human voice quality is as distinctive as the individual fingerprint. The choral conductor must somehow fit these many unique voices into an overall blend of sound.

To ask all members of the choral organization to sing with a single concept of vocal production does not solve the problem of blend nor does such an approach guarantee accurate intonation. On the other hand, to allow all ensemble members to "do their own thing" almost always results in unsatisfactory blend.

If dynamic level is regulated by the weakest member of the organization, a certain kind of blend can be achieved but the results are musically unsatisfactory: an unsupported, breathy tone often results, possibilities for dynamic variety are limited, and a certain blandness of sound develops.

Adapting to Stylistic and Acoustical Requirements

Having recognized the problems of the diversity of individual vocal qualities and power, the conductor must choose a course of action. Fortunately, neither total regimentation nor total freedom must prevail. Instead, it seems reasonable to choose a middle ground that promotes the vocal flexibility and adaptability needed to permit adjustment to the historical stylistic demands of the music and the acoustical demands of the auditorium. Two useful techniques follow.

1. *Experimentation with voice placement within the section.* This leads to an environment in which the acoustical characteristics of neighboring voices work together rather than against each other. The individual singer feels freer and is, therefore, better able to sing in tune and contribute more individual control of the blend within his immediate environment. (This is a feeling similar to that developed by a member of a small ensemble.) This topic will be covered more completely in Chapter 6.
2. *Voice training which develops vocal production without tension.* Such training will enable the singer to obtain the flexibility needed for easy adaptability. This training can occur in the private voice studio, in voice classes, or as a part of the choral rehearsal.

In addition to voice individualities there are the preconception of the individual performer to be considered. Each, because of varied background and training, has a slightly different idea about the contribution desired from him or her.

The Relationship of the Individual Singer to Sectional Balance

Sensitivity of the individual singer to sectional balance is one of the results of free and open tone production combined with an intelligent approach to musicianship. Consideration by both conductor and singer of how the carrying power and quality of one voice interacts with other voices can play an integral part in the development of smoothness of blend within a choral ensemble. Intelligent experimentation by the conductor with the varied qualities of individual voices quite often results in that extra finesse desired for ensemble blend and balance.

SECTIONAL PERSONALITIES OF CHORAL ENSEMBLES

The first step in the proper management of sectional differences is in the judicious selection of the number of singers. A mixed ensemble should generally include more altos and basses than sopranos and tenors. Higher sound frequencies are easier to detect and sound clearer to the ear than lower frequencies. Low pitches tend to be identified by the ear as weak, with an indefinite pitch center.

The higher pitched sections—the tenors and sopranos—can establish a presence in the ensemble with fewer people. Ideally, begin with equal numbers of sopranos and tenors and then add the number of altos and basses necessary to create the desired balance.

In spite of the diversity of individual vocal production these are certain characteristics common within four vocal classifications. The conductor should use a slightly different approach for the development of each section of the ensemble. The techniques used are similar to those of voice-class instructions.

Alto

The alto (usually more mezzo-soprano than contralto) section should be given the highest priority when arranging the choir to achieve overall balance and satisfactory tonal quality. The alto musician has too often been trained to just enjoy "blending" with the remainder of the ensemble. What a waste of talent! If the altos attempt merely to be the blenders in a choral organization, two things may occur:

1. A balance problem becomes noticeable rather immediately.
2. The rich mezzo quality of the alto voice will be missing, and it is this quality that provides the tone enrichment for the foundation of the ensemble.

The influence that the full, rich, warm, mezzo tone quality has on the overall depth of tone of a choir cannot be overstated. Achieving this tone quality, however, can be a challenge. The mezzo voice is perhaps the most difficult instrument to train.

Throughout the middle register a mezzo voice, of necessity, makes slight changes in head and chest register mixtures. This action must become automatic and not involve a lot of muscular manipulations. (The range of notes involved include 4 to 6 semitones—G above middle C to the C octave.) If such "mixing" of tone is not achieved, a "middle-register crisis" for the performer often results. This crisis includes the development of problems such as:

1. lack of control of intonation,
2. a complete change of tonal quality above the middle register,
3. a workable range of less than one octave.

To overcome these problems it is helpful to ask members of the alto section to think of facial head-tone placement similar to that of a soprano. The mezzo-soprano, however, can never be satisfied with localized physical vibration (just in the head or the upper part of the body) so should aim for a fullness of sound which results in large areas of body vibration. If an alto section can think of themselves as big-voice sopranos (which they usually are) they should not have serious problems with the upper register.

Most singers with mezzo voices should also become accustomed to opening the mouth more than other singers so that the fullness of their thicker vocal sounds will have an outlet.

Although the exercise that requires the voice to slide-glide from low to high and back again (and the reverse) is almost a requirement for all beginning and untrained singers, this exercise is most usable and valuable for the mezzo-soprano/alto (Illustration 2). The vowels "ee" [i] and "ay" [e] help keep the voice focused while sliding up and down through the range of the voice.

Illustration 2

ay_____   ee_____

To eventually experience flexibility of a full tessitura, the mezzo-soprano/alto must allow the upper register to originate as a front of the mouth placement vibration—but with mixtures of rather heavy sympathetic body resonance always present.

When the mezzo ensemble member learns to use the most flexible and beautiful of instruments, not only do the tonal qualities of the choral ensemble change dramatically, but generally the vitality with which the music is rehearsed and performed shows noticeable improvement because of increased flexibility and control.

Tenor

The tenor section of a mixed choir ranks second in priority (after the altos) when working towards overall sectional balance. As with the altos, voice production problems can severely limit the effectiveness of the tenor section. Often the young or amateur tenor is quite frustrated, for he thinks of his voice as sounding "squeaky" when he speaks or sings. The amateur tenor, consequently, frequently resorts to production methods which cultivate only the very limited lower register of his vocal range. He soon finds that all such methods lead to tension in the jaw, throat, and tongue. This tension causes severe restriction of workable range, uncontrollable breaks in the voice, and a metallic vocal quality.

Contrary to their perceptions, tenors must be made to appreciate that high male sounds are coveted by the musical world, especially if they are of lyric quality, and that their squeakiness is to be expected as a first step in the voice development process.

The basic goal of the high male voice is to achieve a fully resonated head register vibration. When the feeling of vibration (and to some degree a filling of the head with sympathetic resonation) is present, the tone produced is head tone and not a false voice (falsetto) no matter how light the weight of the voice to the singer.

The tenor, then, works toward adding fullness to the head register voice, whereas the mezzo is adding fullness and color through mixtures of head and chest register classifications. The tenor section as a unit must be persuaded to work for a continual "ring" in the front of the face (eyeballs included). As sympathetic vibrators in other parts of the head and body open, the section should continue to keep the primary "ring" in mind.

Tenors must learn to distinguish, however, between tonal placement "ring" and muscular tension "buzz." A sharpness in pitch coupled with a metallic tone often indicate a muscular tension in the tongue or jaw—"muscular buzz." Complete relaxation in the jaw-tongue area should produce tonal placement ring. Muscular tension in the neck, jaw, and tongue area has an even more devastating effect on the tenor voice than on other voices.

Before leaving the tenors, one other production problem that especially affects tenors should be noted. Mouth movements seem to be more critical for tenors than for either altos or basses. The slightest change in lip formation or internal mouth area seems to influence vowel color significantly. Special attention should be focused on the tenor section when vowel formation requires accurate mouth positions. "Natural" physical feeling for vowel tone coloring can rarely be expected from a tenor section, and must, therefore, be carefully developed.

Bass

One of the most interesting sections in a mixed choir is the bass section. Unlike the tenor, the bass-baritone is usually happy with his voice quality and he likes to use his instrument.

Since he produces a low format sound-wave profile, the bass can feel a large physical area of vibration which allows him to hear his own voice in a dramatic way (William Vennard's *Singing, the Mechanism and the Technic,* Carl Fischer, Inc. 1967). This situation leads, however, to the most serious problem confronting a bass since, from inside his body, the bass singer is likely to inaccurately perceive both the pitch and the quality of his voice.

No one is more shocked by his real quality of sound than a bass listening to his own recorded voice. No ears are less accurate than those of a bass who has not learned to aurally adjust to the outside true pitch. Unless the bass has developed a proper sense of physical vowel placement, his vowel production is likely to be extremely "dark" or muffled. Those dark vowel sounds are often the main causes of the tendency of the bass section to sing flat.

To correct the pitch problem and to improve voice production generally, basses should be given explicit explanations concerning the physical location from which their tone emanates. Unlike the mezzo voice, the chest register sounds are usually already in place awaiting the action of the facial vibrating surfaces. The bass, then, must work on stimulating the primary vibrations of the hard palate and upper teeth to utilize the full-body resonating features of his loud-speaking system.

Basses should experience the "ring" required of the tenor, although generally the area of the vibration is only around the teeth, lips, and gum ridges. Just as the alto must sing with a more open mouth, so must the bass, and for the same reasons.

Sopranos

The sopranos are last, but not necessarily least, in the order of training priorities. Since the sopranos receive the brunt of criticism concerning out-of-tune singing, ugly tone quality, too much vibrato, too little vibrato, screaming sounds, etc., it might seem as though they should be placed higher on the priority list. The soprano voice, however, is probably the easiest to train and the quickest to respond. The soprano section usually can move more easily than other sections toward the "feel" of open sound production because it is more natural for the soprano to physically feel head voice resonance and to quickly rely on such production.

A soprano section experiences the greatest difficulty when the first attempts are made to vocalize in the register above high F, F#, and G. To use a mixing of the head and chest registers and also vowel modification to produce vowel purity at the early stages of ensemble training can be frustrating to both singer and conductor. A concentration on upper register vocal production rapidly brings the soprano a sense of true pitch and flexibility of production.

A placement "ring" at first should be attempted without the use of the "smile," for mouth movement quite often sets up a false sense of tonal sound security. As with the tenors, sopranos soon learn that slight movements in the mouth area create problems in tone coloring. If the mouth is opened too wide, sharpness in pitch will result. If the mouth is opened too long, the pitch will drop.

HOW SECTIONAL PERSONALITY AFFECTS
PLACEMENT OF SECTIONS

As has been previously indicated, the acoustical wave produced by both the higher-pitched soprano and tenor results in a directional, centered and easily projected sound, whereas the lower format of the alto and bass acoustical tone spectrum dictates a less-directional, projected wave, but one rich in quality.

Knowledge of acoustical properties of the tenor and alto instruments should stimulate thought concerning complementary placement of these two sections within the organizational plan of the ensemble. Although the ranges of the altos and tenors are quite similar, the fact that one section (tenor) is made up of tonal projecting instruments and the other (alto) comprised of blending instruments might be reason enough to experiment with placing the two sections near each other.

The tonal spectrum of the mezzo sound profile can reduce the edge of the ringing tenor tone and the natural projecting power of the tenor wave-length. The projecting power of the tenor section quite often picks up the mellow sounds from the alto section to provide more carrying power for those low format voices. The resulting tone-quality enhancement is a vital step towards sectional blend.

Since the soprano acoustical profile promotes an intensity of projecting power and the bass sound which is full of overtones has less carrying power, the soprano and bass sections should be considered for a partnership when organizing a placement chart for an ensemble (see Illustration 3).

Illustration 3

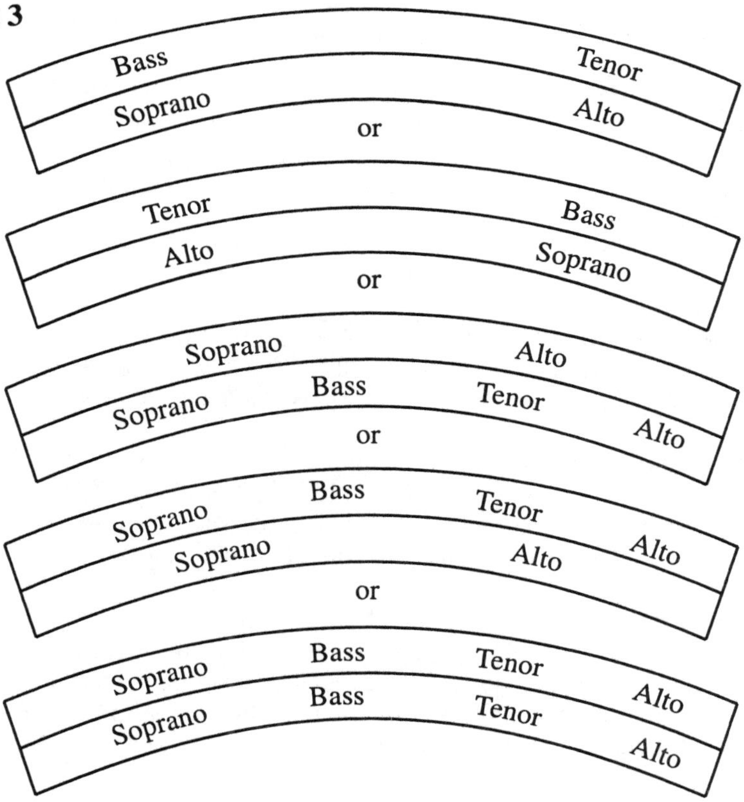

The conductor will find that, while an ensemble is often difficult to balance and blend, the process of achieving this goal will always be a stimulating intellectual challenge and the end results aesthetically satisfying.

The following chapter and Chapter 13 give more detailed solutions for dealing with the voice and sectional individualities discussed in this chapter.

CHAPTER
VI

INFLUENCE OF PERSONNEL PLACEMENT ON CHORAL BLEND AND BALANCE

Most choral conductors would agree that the primary goal of their efforts is to produce a choral sound that is balanced, homogenous, and blended. There is some disagreement, however, as to the best approach for producing such a sound.

Many directors are attracted to textbook, rule-oriented approaches with simple formulas for achieving the desired sound but which, in the end, result in more frustration and confusion than in quality choral performance.

The purpose of this chapter is to examine some of the problems choral conductors face in trying to achieve the best choral sound, and to suggest solutions that are easy to manage, and are fun and effective. Although the principles cited are directed primarily at mixed choirs, most also apply to treble choirs or male choirs.

Two basic problems face most conductors:

1. fitting varying degrees of singer expertise, maturity, and talent into a blended ensemble
2. managing voices in the choir that "stick out" (are larger, more resonant, and more powerful than other voices in the group) while allowing these singers to use their full capacity.

The key to the solution of these problems lies, to a considerable extent, in the way singers are positioned in the ensemble, and the degree to which the conductor is willing to experiment with different sounds produced by various arrangements of personnel. This can sometimes mean the formation of uneven rows, circles, or a total mixing of all personnel within the ranks.

There is little doubt that a certain discipline results when singers are required to sit in the same seats at every rehearsal. However, by enforcing such a rigid discipline, the conductor may be overlooking a valuable opportunity to improve the sound of the group. If the conductor will accept the fact that "musical chairs" can be a valuable rehearsal tool, a process of experimentation can be set into motion that will enhance the quality of the ensemble. If one is going to experiment with personnel placements, several questions arise:

1. Where should different types of voices be placed in the ensemble?
2. What voices complement or clash with each other and how should they be placed?
3. Should choir members be organized along strict sectional lines or should they be formed into clusters of voices situated throughout the choir?

Arrangements of Strong, Average, and Weak Voices

Typically, it is thought that the strong singer (an individual with power to be heard, usually in tune, a fast learner, and quite often an adequate sight reader) should be centrally located within a cluster of weak singers, with the hope that the strong singer's power will somehow be transmitted to the weaker singers surrounding him or her (see Illustration 4).

Illustration 4 **Arrangement to avoid**

S=Strong singer   A=Average singer   W=Weak singer

```
    S S A A A A S S A A A A S S A A
   S W W S W W S W W W W S W S W W
   S A W W W A W W A W W W A A W A
```

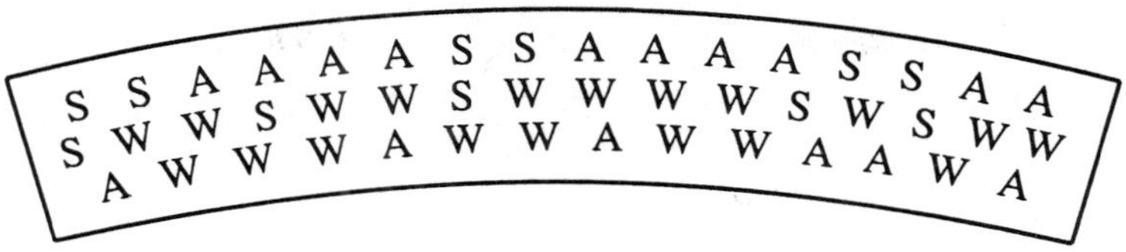

Though sound in theory this approach is deficient when applied to the real world. The strong singer tends to become disoriented, dissatisfied, and bored by his role as a leader or carrier of the weaker performers around him. This role becomes especially onerous to the strong singer if he or she places high value on personal achievement and growth. At the same time, the weaker singers become totally dependent on the strong singer—contributing to a lazy, negative approach to music—and become complacent under the domination of the stronger singer.

Usually, better results can be achieved if singers are placed in "circles" or "zones" of influence within the ensemble, the number of circles depending on the size of the choir and the range of talent among choir members.

Within each circle the stronger singers are surrounded by more average singers, who in turn are placed next to the weaker members of the group (see Illustration 5). This arrangement provides a solid core of singing, and at the same time permits some growth on the part of the most talented members of the choir.

Illustration 5 **Better arrangement**

S = Strong singer   A = Average singer   W = Weak singer

Since the average and less-talented singers are generally placed next to singers of the same ability, they are required to depend on their own intelligence, at least to some degree, to keep up with the group. Yet they are not cut off from the leadership the strongest singers offer.

When placing singers in such an arrangement, however, care should be taken to ensure that the individual singer does not lose vocal identity. Some voice qualities become absorbed or hidden by other voice qualities. Because of this some singers may feel that they are not making a contribution to the group, when in fact their contribution may be considerable.

The singer's perception that he has lost his vocal identity creates "soft spots" in the choir, often manifest as gaps in carrying power within circles or zones in the choir. To promote personal initiative among choir members and to maximize the carrying power of the group, singers should be physically separated to the extent that they can preserve their vocal identities (see Illustration 6).

Illustration 6   **More spacing between singers**

"Carrying Power"

The importance of a choir's carrying power should be emphasized. The ability of a conductor to harness the varying projective capabilities of his singers will determine, to a considerable extent, the quality of sound produced and the number of people in the audience who will hear it.

The human voice, quite simply, is an acoustical loudspeaker system that can be enhanced, blocked, or otherwise affected by other nearby human acoustical systems. Two rows of singers with their own "soaking" loudspeaker systems can steal power very effectively from a strong, vital voice being projected from the back. The carrying power of a choir depends, then, on placing singers in such a fashion that the tone projected by the best singers is not altered or "soaked up" by other members of the choir (see Illustration 7).

Other Voice Quality Problems

Other sound problems within the choir are easily heard. Voice qualities can openly clash, creating harsh, unpleasant sound combinations or tuning discrepancies. Conflicts can occur even between two fine voices. When there are many voices in the choir, voice qualities can be found which will filter out the undesirable sounds.

Those voices that are good filters or blenders may be placed in front of, or next to, the problematic voice, causing the rough edges of the total choral sound to be smoother (see Illustration 7). Discovering good filters is best achieved through experimentation with various arrangements of choir personnel and awakened listening on the part of both singers and conductor. Once the optimal arrangement is found, no singer will feel unproductive or that he or she should hold back because of vocal character.

Illustration 7

C = Vocal carrying power   M = Mature (perhaps strong)   B = Blender
P = Problem voice   V = Vibrato problem

Each singer must be free to use the full range of his or her tonal color and resonating capacity if the choir is going to preserve its flexibility, be capable of performing different styles, and stay in tune. A voice will not add to the quality of the choir if it is in conflict with other voices or if it is swallowed by more dominating sounds.

The conductor should treat each singer as an individual with special talents whose placement in the ensemble is of critical importance to the sound of the choir. In addition, each singer has special needs, of which one is the belief that she or he is contributing to the group and need not fear giving the best he or she has to offer.

The goal of the experimentation-oriented conductor, then, is to create a climate in which personal initiative and discipline are promoted among the singers, and which will also permit the creativity and sensitivity of each singer to surface for the benefit of the total choral sound.

Arranging Singers in Rows

Besides taking care in deciding who is placed next to whom in the choir, the conductor must also be careful in choosing which singers are placed in which rows.

The First Row: It is generally wise to place the more vocally mature voices in the front row. The singers in the front row can be expected to set the tonal color of the choir as a whole and cover, to some degree, the less-refined sounds produced by the more vocally immature voices elsewhere in the choir.

In order for the tonal color to be set by the front row, however, it must contain singers who project well. These usually will be singers with formal training or with natural carrying power, which are criteria for front-row selection.

The Second Row: This row in a choral ensemble tends to blend and balance the front row. The degree to which this is accomplished depends on how second-row voices are arranged to act on first-row voices.

The second row should receive the most attention in the arrangement of choir personnel during rehearsal. It should be the major point of focus in the conductor's experimentation with the sound of the choir. Singers who blend well, are in tune, and are musically intelligent should be given highest consideration for the second row.

The Third Row: Persons selected for the third row generally should be those singers with some vocal characteristic that adversely affects the blend of the group. Included here would be those voices that are too huge and must be slimmed by other voices placed to the side and the front. Also included would be those voices with such a vibrato that they cannot easily be assimilated into the sound of the ensemble.

Some care should be taken that the third row does not take on the reputation as the "dummy line." The filtering effect of the first two rows, nonetheless, makes the third row especially suitable for voices that are difficult to blend as previously shown in Illustration 7.

Other Rows: The same basic principles of choir organization apply to ensembles using more than three rows. The first two or three rows will act as filter on the choir as a whole and will require special attention by the conductor. The remaining rows will not perform such a specialized function, but they should not be neglected. The director may want to create a second series of circles of influence in the back rows on the basis of the carrying power and quality of sound of those singers.

Another Possibility: Placement of Choir in Quartets

To get everyone in a choir in a position to hear most of the other voice parts, it is helpful to place personnel in quartets throughout the choir. To be most effective in promoting hearing, perhaps one should not just place a soprano, alto, tenor, bass quartet next to a similar quartet but provide a mix of tenor, alto, soprano, bass next to the usual quartet placement. Just a small change in arrangement (see Illustration 8) can bring more of a variety of sound to the singer's ears, which is always healthy for the individual performer.

Illustration 8

S = Soprano   A = Alto   T = Tenor   B = Bass

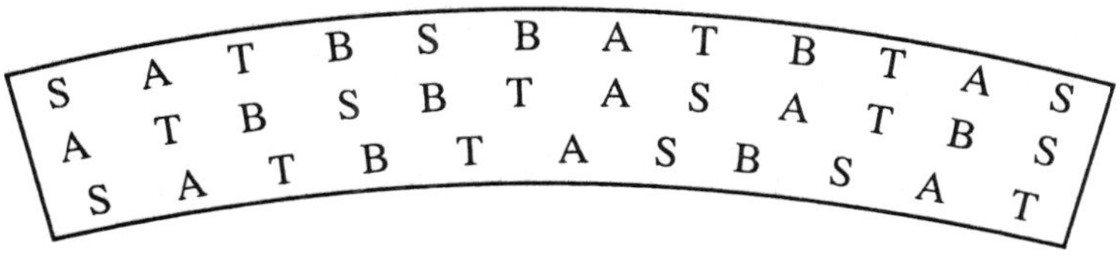

This arrangement will work well if the singers are fairly secure. Insecure singers may still be placed next to others of their own parts until they develop more security.

The conductor will find it necessary to adjust conducting techniques somewhat to handle the quartet arrangement. It is hard to define the communication that goes on between choir and conductor in this situation, but a little experimentation with techniques will bring results.

One of the positive results of this situation is that individual responsibility increases dramatically. Each singer must become prepared to accept signals applicable to his or her voice section.

Many singers who have experienced this arrangement prefer it to all others. Some singers never become comfortable with it.

Some Cautions

Perhaps it would be well to add a few words of caution to the conductor interested in using an experimentation-oriented approach as described in this chapter.

First, such placement experimentation must evolve and be flexible, from the first rehearsal to the final concert. Adjustments must be made throughout that time as individual voices develop and as physical surroundings change. If one waits until just before a concert to experiment, it will probably be too late to accomplish what is needed, and the singers will not feel comfortable. With differing psychological approaches I have used these methods to some extent with all ages and types of singing groups.

Second, be careful not to substitute "gimmicks" for a sound rehearsal discipline. The techniques described should not be used simply because they are fun or provide novelty in an otherwise sterile rehearsal routine. The ideas may be different, but the ultimate goal of the ensemble conductor is the same: producing a sound that is disciplined, and providing a choral experience that is meaningful both to performers and listeners.

Third, the conductor should be careful that he or she does not develop lazy ears personally or allow personal discipline to slip.

Fourth, it is helpful to have a seating chart constructed before entering the rehearsal and begin with people seated according to the chart. Changes may be made throughout the rehearsal with hand signals which will not interrupt the flow of the rehearsal. The singers should be instructed to assume the same positions at the beginning of the next rehearsal that they held at the end of the previous rehearsal unless a new seating chart is provided.

Fifth, whether the experimental method outlined above is successful rests, to a considerable degree, on the skill and dedication of the conductor. He or she must to be able to recognize different voices and analyze how their placement in the choir will affect the overall sound. Equally important, the conductor must be willing to expend the effort necessary to identify different voices and find their optimal location in the ensemble.

With expertise, all of the above can be accomplished without actually taking time away from the rehearsal. ("Musical chairs" while singing can be fun!)

CHAPTER VII

CHORAL AND INSTRUMENTAL COMBINATIONS

A few ideas will be presented in this chapter to develop greater vocal efficiency and create better stylistic concepts when performing literature for instruments and choir. A knowledge of historical background and musical practices is certainly required to perform an older cantata or oratorio. An acquaintance with contemporary compositions is desired if the work is new. With style in mind, evaluate the different projection characteristics of individual instruments as well as vocal sections.

Choir With Orchestra

The typical arrangement of musicians when performing a large instrumental-choral composition is the placement of the orchestra in front of the choir whose members are standing on risers. This arrangement has been in vogue for many years and will certainly continue to be used. One problem with this arrangement is the difficulty encountered by the choir in its efforts to project choral sound through the full spectrum of instrumental sound (unless the instrumentalists are in a pit).

When an orchestra is the instrumental medium, the tonal timbre of altos and violas are quite compatible, and cellos and choir basses match beautifully. The result, quite often, is that the altos and basses cannot be heard while the high register of the sopranos and tenors carries their voices through the orchestra.

If the individual orchestral members play well, the singers may find it difficult to make themselves heard. Even huge voices can be tamed by instruments which possess a similar sound. Smaller voices have very little chance of being important contributors to the performance. Since the story line is in the choral score, the vocal performer strongly feels the responsibility to communicate both the text and the emotional impact of the composition and is frustrated when this becomes impossible.

It sometimes becomes necessary to alter beautiful choral ensemble balance when balancing choir and orchestra. The orchestral instruments, especially the strings, accept choral sounds very easily and will often take the edge off voices which tend to "stick out" under ordinary circumstances. Voices that are usually difficult to fit into an ensemble because of extreme efficiency in carrying power are of utmost importance when considering ways to produce a curtain of tone that will cut through an orchestra (see Vennard's *Singing, the Mechanism and the Technic*, Carl Fisher, Inc., 1967). These voices with naturally good production should be placed in the front row of the ensemble (a new experience for many of these usually fine singers).

To add to excellence in individual carrying quality, use mixed quartets or alternate voice parts (tenor and alto, for example) at the front of the choir. This front line vocal defensive unit will set the acoustical pattern for the full choir. It is, therefore, only the first and perhaps the second line of the choir that will need to be in altered part positions. The remaining rows can fit into favorite choir positioning.

The strongest voices, therefore, should be used toward the front of the ensemble when performing with orchestra; voices that blend easily should be used on the front rows only to separate voices that absolutely will not fit together. (Since singers who blend well feel more comfortable when they can hear themselves produce tone, they will perform better when they can hear their individual contribution. They may have to make a bit of a sacrifice to sing in the front row under these conditions.)

As an example, an ensemble might be organized as in Illustration 9 for a typical oratorio performance.

Illustration 9

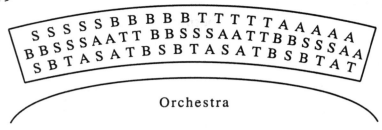

Orchestra

As is quickly discovered, ensembles with few tenors and basses are able to promote maximum efficiency from this altered arrangement. The altos, however, are the performers who reap the most benefit from the placement. Rather than merely blending with each other and the strings, each singer is producing as a soloist and, therefore, projecting a most important part of the composition.

A further suggestion for gaining more choral sound when performing with an orchestra is to extend the choral ensemble lines behind and to the sides of the orchestra if possible as shown in Illustration 10. As has been suggested previously, some voice patterns tend to absorb other voice profiles. If one can separate the different projections of sound, carrying power is increased.

Illustration 10

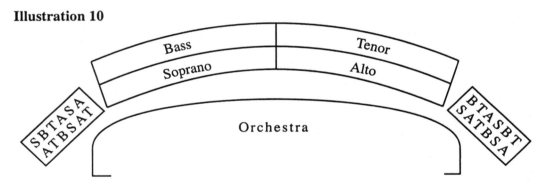

To require an ensemble member to look between two string basses or to be in danger of a timpani mallet blow is probably asking greater dedication than should be expected. Some flexibility in placement may be necessary to avoid such problems.

Another suggestion for helping the choir sing through the orchestra is to demand more emphasis on the consonants. Since this disturbs the flow of sound and brings the voice placement forward, the tone is able to cut through the orchestra more successfully.

The ideas raised in the preceding paragraphs will have very little impact upon those conductors who have 500 excellent voices to call upon when an oratorio is to be performed. However, for those who do not have such numbers and who may be dealing with immature voices, experimentation with basic acoustical principles will lead to more satisfying performances.

Choir With Brass

Now, a few rather simple suggestions for small ensemble instrumental and choral combinations. A brass instrument and a voice are never equal no matter how large the voice. The brass player always wins! When using any brass combination with choir, the instruments, as much as possible, should play toward another instrument and never toward the audience (Illustration 11).

Illustration 11

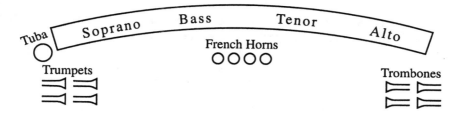

Choir With Woodwinds

If woodwind instruments are the accompanying medium, the only consideration deals with the blending of voices and instruments. For example, if flutes and sopranos have attractive duets, place the flutes near the sopranos. If the basses and the bass clarinet do not tune well together, place the bass clarinet away from the bass section of the choir.

Choir With Percussion

When a choir is performing with percussion, problems arise. For the sake of balance it would be ideal to place the instruments behind the singers, but the players would not be able to see the conductor! The best placement for bass drums, timpani, snare drums and cymbals is, therefore, at the edge of the choir formation.

The effect of striking percussion hardware interrupts a choir's sound curtain to the point that, if they are placed in front of the choir, the acoustical waves are so ragged the choir balance is disturbed and diction is greatly modified. To keep a choir tone curtain intact, percussion can be most effectively used, for both choir and percussion, outside the choral acoustical wave pattern.

Pitch-producing instruments, such as xylophones and bells, combine well with choral sound. These instruments offer few problems in the area of total balance and can, therefore, be placed in front of the choir (Illustration 12).

Illustration 12

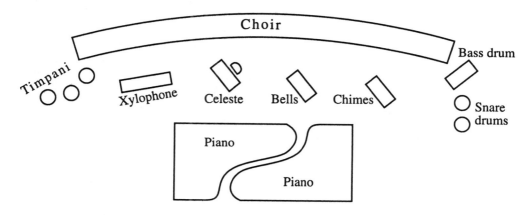

Choir With Chamber Orchestra

Generally, few problems exist with balance when a chamber orchestra and choir perform together. If one does encounter balance problems, the following ideas may be helpful.

1. If risers are used for the choir, place the choir as high on the risers as possible.
2. If the choir is quite small use one row rather than multiple rows.
3. For *pianissimos,* use fewer string players for dramatic contrast.

Choir With Band

Bands and choirs can make beautiful music together, but often the choir loses all sense of contribution to the beauty of the performance since the sound of the band can easily overwhelm the human voices. If room is available, the easiest way of setting up for a band and choir performance is to place the ensembles side by side. If such space is not possible then experiment with the general pattern shown in Illustration 13.

Illustration 13

Arrows indicate direction instruments are facing

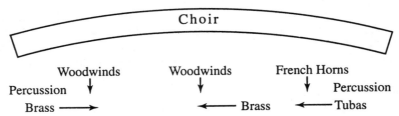

If the singers are quite immature, the brass should be asked to play one level softer than indicated in the score. This solution will be more acceptable to the instrumentalists than one in which they are subjected to a complete performance of *pianissimo* blowing.

Instrumentalists can be more proficient and produce fuller sounds at a younger age than can vocalists. The vocal instrument does not mature until the body surrounding the instrument completes the maturing process. This fact has to be taken into consideration when placing choral and instrumental ensembles together. The potential in educational development is far too great, however, for any choral ensemble to avoid participation with instrumental ensembles in performance.

Experimentation with the sound-carrying qualities of individual instruments and voices can produce a most satisfying musical result for both performer and listener.

CHAPTER VIII

BREATHE FROM THE DIAPHRAGM . . . WHERE?

Most singers have been instructed frequently to "breathe from the diaphragm." Many amateur choir members, however, have some difficulty deciding how one breathes from an elusive, non-feeling part of the body called a diaphragm. The diaphragm is discussed in many books and articles, but no one covers the topic better than William Vennard in his book, *Singing, the Mechanism and the Technic* (Carl Fischer, 1967). Vennard describes the diaphragm as a "large dome-shaped muscle which divides the trunk into two parts, with the lungs and heart above and the rest of the viscera below. Actually, it is almost a double dome, with the stomach and spleen under the left dome and the liver under the right. The heart is in the middle above, and the two domes are separated by the backbone."

Since the diaphragm technically is not an active working muscle, its contraction and expansion must be controlled by abdominal muscles. Basically, while singing, the chest is held high, the shoulders are relaxed, and the abdominal muscles pull the dome of the diaphragm down and outward to allow air to enter the lungs. Contraction of these muscles in a controlled manner pushes the air out of the lungs. These same muscles control energy for starting and stopping the tone, for accents and for breath-budgeting. One should begin, therefore, the training of the breathing apparatus by developing control of the abdominal muscles.

Training the Muscles

As any athlete must work to gain needed muscular strength and control, so must the singer train essential muscles to gain strength and control. The athlete suffers some discomfort, and so will the typical performer in an ensemble. An athletic trainer will isolate certain areas for the athlete to work on; the conductor of a choir can do the same for the singers. For example, since the muscles which control the diaphragmatic dome are the same muscles as those used for a "belly laugh" or a "gasp" when one is frightened, a possible beginning exercise (to locate the necessary muscles) would be to instruct all ensemble members to place their hands behind their heads at the neck (to keep chests from dropping), pant in a most seductive, reckless manner, and then turn such panting into vocalized laughing.

Even in the midst of the first throes of abdominal muscle training, long fully-energized tones should be encouraged while using proper vowel production. (The control, or lack of control, exhibited can be quite amusing at times.)

Just as physical exercise must become a daily habit for those wishing to tone the body muscles, so should specific breathing exercises suggested by the conductor become a habit for the singer. The conductor can also devise exercises to be interspersed within the rehearsal that will address specific problems in the music and at the same time enhance muscle development. See Illustrations 14 and 15.

Illustration 14

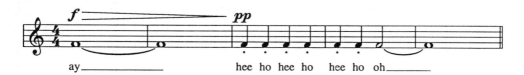

Illustration 15
A "bouncing belly" syndrome for runs. No "h"—just a light stomach bounce for each note.

ay - - -   oh - - - -   ee_____

Exercises such as these will keep the concept of full-time use of the abdominal muscles before the choir, and promote physical ease of producing tone.

In addition to regularly scheduled exercises many other opportunities may be created. For instance, ensemble members can greet each other outside the rehearsal hall with original exercises designed for almost any occasion (staccato "hello's," accented name identification, a spoken sentence with crescendo and decrescendo added, or, perhaps, the holding of a name or word until all breath is exhausted).

Muscle Techniques for Tone Control

Soon the choir members will gain some feeling of how the muscles work to provide more air for the lungs and greater control of this air. At this stage, the conductor must ask for a transfer of these new techniques to greater reliance on the breathing apparatus for all tone control.

Such a transfer is not easy for the singer to immediately implement. There are often temporary problems with pitch and with consistent vocal placement. The results, however, will be considered worth the short-lived pain when choir members, one by one, begin to achieve tonal flexibility. As proper techniques are developed, the fact will become evident that correct breathing and breath control is the foundation of fine ensemble control, flexibility, and beautiful tone production.

Breathing exercises that might help during a period of transference include the following:

1. While gradually decreasing in volume, try to maintain strength in the abdominal muscles (keeping a fullness in the mid-section of the body).

2. Make the abdominal muscles alternately expand and contract while maintaining a steady tone or moving up and down a scale pattern.

3. While practicing choral materials ask the singers to try to end each phrase with better posture than at the beginning of the phrase. This should be done with a feeling of strength in the abdominal area rather than a feeling of muscular collapse.

4. If a short composition is memorized, a sing-through of the composition with each member of the ensemble holding his or her hands above the head will help keep the muscles, lungs, and rib cage in usable positions. (This technique can also be used with exercises designed for other purposes, such as faulty pitch problems.)

5. The back of the rehearsal chair can be very effectively used as a way to feel and develop muscle expansion in the lower back area (Illustration 16).

Illustration 16

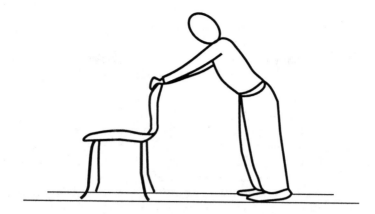

The diaphragmatic muscle must be the servant of many muscles before it will control both lung capacity and power. A degree of tonal flexibility, the power to project tone and the creation of beauty of tone can only be achieved when all sounds are successfully controlled by the breathing apparatus.

CHAPTER
IX

VOWEL COLORING AND HISTORICAL IMPLICATIONS

It is presumed that music of each time period has its own distinctive sound qualities. Some aspects of this sound are created by using certain tone colors that are appropriate for the music of that particular historical period. Traditionally, conductors have learned historical style/tone relationships but have received very little information concerning vocal manipulation necessary to meet historical requirements.

There is a danger that, when one has been carefully trained to be style conscious, concepts of vocal energy and communicative ability will become low priority. Conversely, when no emphasis is placed on stylistic concepts, musical performance may become an accumulation of monochromatic sounds which soon produce a dull sameness for both performer and listener. Compromise must be considered when trying to balance interesting historical tonal ideas with excitement in tonal production.

The most important problem to be addressed concerning vocal manipulation for historical style requirements is that of keeping the vocal instrument healthy and able to produce open, free sounds.

The Responsibility of the Choral Conductor for the Vocal Health of the Ensemble

I believe that the conductor must know the inner workings of the vocal instrument in order to determine, or help the singer determine, the outside limits of the voice as tonal concepts are altered to fit historical style requirements. How often have we, as ensemble members, experienced the wrath of the listening composer who cares not for the health of the singers' voices but only for the single performance monument to his or her composing talent. Singers have also experienced the barbed attack by the master conductor who demands more volume than the voice can offer when performing an oratorio. We, the choral specialists, must be qualified to determine whether the ensemble members are shirking their duty or are instead using their voices with the maximum productive efficiency. (See Chapter 7 for some solutions for these problems.)

Rehearsal organization certainly is important when vocal health is a top priority. The conductor should be aware that a full rehearsal on any single vowel will create vocal tension. Also, keeping singers out of their normal range for too long a time will promote vocal tiredness and tension—even when singing prescribed vowels.

We have no other recourse but to accept some of the responsibility for the vocal health of our singers. The marriage of our goals for choral literature style requirements to our knowledge of what can be expected of the vocal mechanism eventually requires compromise.

Tonal Concepts for Early Music Eras

Vocal Ramifications

If the musicologist/conductor wishes no vibrato (straight tone production) for early music materials, he or she should realize that the vocal mechanism must make certain physical changes which will tend to cut off a part of the total loudspeaker area. This adjustment will affect the carrying power of the voice as well as the workable tessitura range.

When the vocal instrument is asked to produce a straight sound without vibrato:
1. The originating placement moves toward the back of the mouth.
2. A degree of muscle tightness is necessarily exerted in the vocal cage area to "thin" the natural vibrato tonal spectrum.

3. A degree of vocal efficiency is therefore lost when the tone vibrator (vocal folds) cannot easily work in cooperation with the loudspeaker system (mouth area).
4. The breathing apparatus must also labor to compress the air for a tight, tense vibrator system.

One result of all this extra muscular tension is a loss of true pitch in the higher register and a rather "metallic" tone which offers very little variety of color. Perhaps a more frightening result for many singers is the fact that the instrument often cannot take the wear and tear of continual tension. After a certain length of time (varying with the individual singer) the result of this continual tension may possibly be a muscular reaction which will produce either a very wide, uncontrollable vibrato or a severe loss of control during register breaks. The conductor should be especially conscious of these problems when working with young and/or untrained voices.

It must be understood, however, that quite a number of trained performers can stand the tension and are able to use the full vocal ability without damage to the instrument. There is no way whereby one can determine whether or not his or her voice will be able to withstand the rigors of "straight-tone" performance other than through experience.

The difficulties encountered by a singer in making adjustments in the vocal mechanism while alternating between the vibrato-restricted tone and a full, open and well-placed tone should be understood and carefully considered. It is possible to attain a musical-line transparency in early literature which allows the performer a degree of ease in adjusting the vocal mechanism. This procedure is not as complex as one might think, but conceptual compromise may have to be adopted.

A Conceptual Compromise

It is best that the ensemble member not be told to consciously restrict vibrato or tone in order to achieve historical style. Instead, a consistent rehearsing of varying vowel colors rather than texts will help to achieve desired results. Changes will probably occur naturally in the vocal mechanism and the singer will soon become adept in voice manipulation without restrictive tension.

There is a method which will not completely satisfy the "purists" but which should fulfill their musical requirements for transparency and agility. A forward production of the vowel "oo" lightens the tone considerably and if used often in rehearsal tends to "slim" the vibrato to almost a straight sound production. For example, the "oo" can be used instead of the text until the music is well executed. Then the text can be added with similar quality, but with the expectation of returning to the "oo" if the tone becomes too heavy.

Tonal beauty is present as a result of full usage of the loudspeaker system and vocal cage area. Placement of the "oo" must be conceived as tending toward the forwardness of the vowel "ee" and not as a combination of the "oh" and the "oo" vowels. Tone will then remain light, resulting in excellent mobility and, for most singers, easy tuning.

Because the singer is not working to overcome tension in the vocal apparatus caused by a conscious straightening of the tone, breath control is more easily achieved and is more efficient. The little vibrato left in the voice is barely noticeable by either listener or performer. The tone produced by the "oo" vowel tends to be a bit warm (never metallic), lyric (not piercing), usable (but not restricted in range), and an aesthetically pleasing compromise tone (rather than a completely straight "white" sound).

Applications of Vowel Colors for Historical Interpretations of Other Time Periods

The use of different vowel colors will aid in presenting historical interpretations for later time periods while still protecting vocal health and flexibility.

Baroque Era

A tonal approach to early Baroque might be enhanced by rehearsing the ensemble on a German umlaut "ü" [y] to add more color and just a bit of vibrato to the tone production.

When considering later Baroque compositions a German umlaut "ö" [o] could be rehearsed to add color and musical interest. The tonal concept is that of free and colorful sound but not of a widely vibrated tone.

Classic Era

When literature from the Classic era (Haydn, Mozart, etc.) is in the rehearsal stage, the vowel "ah" might be used if the desire is for more openness of sound but with a retention of flexibility. The "open" vowel "ah" [a] should not be mixed with the "covered" vowel "aw" [ɔ] color if clarity is desired when performing this music. An aesthetically pleasing amount of vibrato will be present if the open "ah" is used as a tone-color device.

Romantic Era

The ensemble member must, of course, use the full rich voice for materials from the Romantic literature. The adjustment of the voice for full resonation efficiency is easier if the instrument does not have to shift the muscular tension from extreme tightness to full efficiency.

The "oh" [o] vowel is of great value in training the voice for a richness of sound with full vibrato. A problem of flat intonation, however, can haunt the conductor who doesn't mix the "oh" with a dose of "ah." A performer is inclined to enjoy the thickness of the "oh" sound to the exclusion of proper tonal placement. As soon as the frontal placement "buzz" leaves the singer, the pitch becomes flat.

Modifications in Historical Tonal Requirements to Achieve Performing Goals

Slight variations in the vocal sounds (as previously suggested) emanating from a choral ensemble can add to the excitement for both the listener and the performer. These slight changes can, at the same time, satisfy our desires for being reasonably accurate and sensitive to the historical background of the composition.

Music performance must always, however, have the element of communication as its highest goal. Too often a sense of boredom occurs in both listener and performer when one coldly calculates the decibels of loudness and the number of vibrations per second to determine the tonal concept singers used during Bach's presence on earth. We all too quickly place the tonal character of one culture into the musical framework of another culture and call such an approach accurate. We are apt to forget that we do not have recordings made by Palestrina and the ensembles of that period, and that he probably did not care exclusively about the tonal purity of performance.

Choral conductors of the twentieth century are fortunate to have access to the results of a large amount of scholarship and research concerning music history and are fortunate that they can aim for historical interest through vocal manipulation. The conductor and the singer, however, should never feel as though older literature was for another time and cannot be performed today without great tonal restraints. If a vibrato accidentally appears when performing a composition by Vittoria, but the text, the harmonic beauty and the musical understanding seem to be present, the performance will be an exciting adventure for all (and probably Vittoria would not greatly disapprove).

Tonal Requirements for Contemporary Classical Music

Contemporary music presents many exciting possibilities for the conductor and choir, for we can often use our full repertoire of vocal colors while performing an individual composition. This music depends greatly on either a wide variety of tonal color or lack of any color. The conductor can often identify Baroque inclinations, Renaissance clarity, or Ars Antiqua characteristics when studying the music of the twentieth century. In fact, one of the several rewards gained from performing contemporary music is that of the many opportunities for individual experimentation with vocal sounds.

As always, care must be taken to preserve the healthy conditions of the instrument. Once again, compromise is in all probability the means to that end.

CHAPTER

A FEW THOUGHTS ABOUT REHEARSAL ORGANIZATION

Few choir directors would concede that they have all the rehearsal time necessary to train an ensemble. An efficient, well-run rehearsal, therefore, is a requirement for excellence in education and performance. The suggestions that follow are probably not new ideas, but some may have been forgotten as other urgent matters intrude on the mind.

Business Requirements

Announcements during rehearsal are essential to the well-being of the choir personnel. An efficient order of business approach should be used. Since directors are notorious for a lack of organizational clarity and brevity, procedures should be implemented to have announcements prepared and presented by ensemble members with the director acting as timekeeper and moderator.

It is suggested that announcements include only business pertaining to the choir and that the schedule for such business activity vary from rehearsal to rehearsal. Rather strict time limitations should be placed upon those who have been given the responsibility of providing necessary information to the ensemble.

Since the care of the printed music is the responsibility of each ensemble member, measures must be implemented to insure that each singer assumes such responsibility. If music is rarely studied outside of class, a music cabinet with individual names of singers printed on each slot is an efficient method of organization. (Each singer will then use the same copy at each rehearsal.)

If, however, a paid or volunteer librarian is available, a part of the librarian's duties may be that of putting together individual folders—one of which can then be checked out by each ensemble member. The folders should contain a sheet explaining the cost of each item within the folder; each performer must assume responsibility for the music by signing a form stating such.

No matter what library system is used, the individual singer should be encouraged to write in the score in pencil when suggested by the director or when judged helpful by the singer. The same score must be used by the same singer throughout all rehearsals and performance.

Planning and Pacing of Rehearsal Time

An efficient conductor, no matter how experienced, will go into rehearsal with specific time allotments for each composition to be rehearsed. Flexibility in realizing the set plan of action is the name of the game, however, for one composition could require less rehearsal time than originally planned, and another composition may not rehearse comfortably during that particular rehearsal. A change of time scheduling must be instantly implemented to accommodate these altered requirements. No apologies are needed for a change of scheduling or for misreading the time it will take an ensemble to work out a composition.

Singers who know how to do so should be encouraged to warm up before coming to rehearsal. Any time spent in warm-up at the beginning of rehearsal should be designed to correct vocal problems common to members of that particular group as previously diagnosed by the conductor.

Rehearsals should begin at the designated time whether or not all ensemble members are in position and should end on the required second. If possible, the rehearsal should begin and end with the ensemble singing as a unit. It is suggested that the beginning

38

repertoire be easy on the voice, and perhaps be sung on an "mmm" hum or an "oo" vowel to warm-up the voices.

It may be more effective to dismiss the choir in the middle of a well-performed phrase, or word, than to try to finish the composition in a rush with a less-than-serious approach to the composition at hand. The idea that the rehearsal always must end with a light "pop" melody is probably not well-founded.

The conductor, by example and attitude, influences the choir to be organized and ready for serious rehearsal. Quite often the ensemble member reacts to evidence of serious organization shown by the director with a more disciplined rehearsal attitude.

Relaxation and Humor

Relaxation and levity throughout the rehearsal are excellent tools, but only if the approach is taken that relaxation follows intense work and levity provides relief from a highly disciplined rehearsal.

Choir members and the conductor might joke about Mozart or Brahms (whose feelings can no longer be hurt), but never should any singer be allowed to laugh at a fellow performer—no matter how glaring the mistake. One must learn to experience empathy with others rather than immediately criticize. At the same time, mediocrity must never become an acceptable standard.

The conductor often needs to make rapid decisions relative to cut-off time for humor from the troops, the need for a change of pace in the rehearsal, and the determination of the boundary line of good taste in humor. It is doubtful that using contrived "cuteness" has ever worked for any conductor except to place the rehearsal discipline at a very low and ineffective level. Originality in levity and a controlled relaxation approach, however, are most desirable and, at times, almost necessary for effective accomplishment of musical goals.

Posture

To ensure proper breath support most of us have been instructed to require excellent posture from our ensemble members. This is a most positive and desirable approach. If, however, such excellence in posture is a constant demand, the ensemble member can tire. A rehearsal conductor might, therefore, institute a discipline which allows the performer to relax while instructions are being given but which requires an immediate return to a correct body positioning when rehearsal performance resumes. It should be noted that nothing can substitute for the standing position when proper vocal breathing/body coordination is desired.

Choice of Repertoire

Choral conductors tend to be a bit too sensitive when they hear rumblings about their choice of "heavy" music, and questioning from both students and parents as to why music "we all like" isn't placed before the ensemble in greater quantities. The choral specialist often "gives in" because of very little consideration for, or understanding of, the educational merits of studying and performing excellent literature is recognized by parents, churches, administrators or even other professional musicians. If not persistent, the choir will be relegated to providing "happy time" for the local school, church or community ensemble organizations.

Yes, life can be rather lonely for the choral specialist who decides to battle the prevailing "fun" music syndrome, but it seems we must do battle for our rights as legitimate musicians. The orchestra conductor feels duty-bound to perform traditional music literature which strengthens each ensemble member's ability to expertly handle the chosen instrument. Why should the choral conductor not feel the same compulsion for the same reason? Vocal instrument strength, flexibility, and fluency will not be helped by squeaking stylized vocal sounds into a "revved-up" loudspeaker system.

Only music which challenges, coupled with a conductor who knows how to meet the challenge, can effect positive change in the vocal abilities of the ensemble member. This can lead eventually to a heightened and advanced stage of learning excitement.

Rehearsals need music of all classifications to satisfy a truly educational experience. The choral conductor learns to live with singer unrest in the hope that positive value judgments will eventually develop and prevail.

The Accompanist

The accompanist is a key link to the successful rehearsal. If a conductor is fortunate enough to have a sensitive, technically proficient individual with a pleasant personality as accompanist, the rehearsal runs about 60 times smoother than if the accompanying artist is a cold "note plunker."

There is a danger, however, that a conductor will put so much trust in an excellent accompanist that the accompanying artist is allowed to set tempos (which is done very willingly). This signals "danger ahead" for the conductor's beat can no longer be used to interpret the music.

For more extensive information about accompanying, see Chapter XV.

It is sheer delight to be a part of a harmonious and professional rehearsal team. The choir can hardly keep from being affected in a positive way while observing such a team in action.

CHAPTER XI

PROGRAMMING: A DEMANDING ART

The development of the drama of an oratorio or cantata performance is a joy to experience. It is also simple to put the text into printed program form. Everything has been organized by the composer, and all a choral conductor must do is make the printed program visually attractive and include all names of performers and other relevant details.

The typical choral ensemble does not live by oratorio alone, however, but rather by performing a variety of musical styles. Concern about an interesting organization for performing a diversified program is of paramount importance to the conducting artist. Excellence in creative programming is indeed a demanding art.

The ideas most of us have obtained through reading, in university classes, or in a clinic situation are excellent and workable. Usable ideas we may have learned and experienced possibly include the following:

1. Work for proper key alignments throughout the program. (Compositions which clash in key structure should not be used next to each other.)
2. Begin and end the performance with big, loud and fast tempo compositions.
3. Do not program many slow-moving compositions in sequence.
4. Strive for visual appeal as well as aural interest.
5. Try to create a fast pace when programming in order to maintain audience interest.
6. Consider using a central theme as one interesting way of organizing a program.

One must program carefully within the basic ideas enumerated above, however, in order to accomplish the desired stream of communication between choir and audience. It is necessary to avoid randomly performing one number after another, no matter how well-chosen the music literature or how fine the performing organization. In this situation the ensemble and conductor often revert to either becoming "stiff and formal" or to a "cutesy" approach to stage deportment. Neither satisfies the need for artistic programming.

When attending a theater presentation or a movie, the individual usually experiences a wide range of emotional reaction. Perhaps when putting together a program using a variety of styles, the conductor should explore the range of emotional stimuli in the chosen literature.

"Ave Verum Corpus" by William Byrd can be a beautiful, touching experience for both the performer and listener, but not if it is preceded by "I Bought Me a Cat" by Aaron Copland (no reflection on either composition). A suggestion might be to perform the "Laetentur Coeli" by William Byrd as preparation before experiencing the "Ave Verum Corpus." The next problem, then, becomes one of bringing all listeners and performers away from the ethereal moments connected with the "Ave Verum Corpus" without emotional shock. One might decide to perform another slow, but contrasting, composition from the same period to ease the emotional transition toward another goal.

That next goal might be just purely entertainment. Certainly there is nothing wrong with entertaining literature being an integral part of the program if the audience has been prepared for the change.

Such elements as tempo and key change can never be overlooked when putting a program together, but the most critical analysis should be applied to the dramatic impact of each segment within the program format.

A program combining materials of all types and from many historical periods can possess a natural, built-in dramatic interest if the compositions are presented with historical sequence in mind. The tonal transparency of the Renaissance period moves smoothly into the changing tone color of the Baroque era, which proceeds beautifully into the searching for tonal richness and shading possibilities of the Romantic period. All of the above lead quite logically to experimentation with varieties of tonal concepts to satisfy the contemporary appetite.

If both religious and secular texts are used for general programming, one approach is to program the sacred texts in historical sequence and then offer the same sequence with the secular texts after an intermission.

Programming according to historical gradation, however, will occasionally fail to satisfy all basic requirements for dramatic interest—especially when a variety of choir personnel arrangements within the hall are indicated. The presence of too much physical movement from location to location during a concert can detract from a continuing thread of dramatic intent.

For example, if a portion of the concert is given to polychoral compositions by Gabrieli and Schütz, such materials might be performed at the first of the program, followed by a section of Renaissance motets, thereby eliminating one physical move by the choir. Historical fidelity is not maintained, but in all probability the dramatic force of the program will prove more effective without long pauses filled with the sound of thundering feet hitting the risers.

As with all conductors who have been in the business for many years, I have many stories and experiences to share concerning this most fascinating profession. It is not necessary to give a profusion of such stories. One story, however, will help to make a point about the frustrations that can be experienced when putting together a program to engage the audience, rather than just entertain.

When selecting literature for a rather extensive tour planned for the spring, I decided to program an avant-garde work, "The Vision" by Dale Jergenson (composed in 1971). This is a most interesting score which requires the choir to circle the audience and for seven dramatically-inclined readers to line up at the front of the hall. The text is called "Big Fat Hairy Vision of Evil" written by Lawrence Ferlinghetti and is a rather dramatic episode on what one might experience when drugged. No singing is done but many hissing sounds and harsh interruptions are expressed by the choir. The soloists provide a sing-song disconnected array of ideas turned into sentences, some complete, some not.

It was my idea that programming such a composition would offer a different type of interest during the secular part of the concert. It did! I lost the attention of the first audience completely after performing the number—the rest of the secular numbers were useless.

A change in the order of the program was made before the second concert, and again I lost the attention of the audience—the composition frightened them! Finally, I programmed the composition at the end of the sacred section of the concert, right before the intermission. This placement seemed to give members of the audience time to recuperate and then to enjoy the remainder of the program. Even though the composition provides a thoughtful moral consideration, it cannot be classified sacred in text or setting. The only place for this selection, however, seemed to be at the finish of the sacred portion of the concert.

Interesting and effective programming, though a challenging and difficult art form, should receive careful attention.

CHAPTER
XII

SIGHT-READING

What the music world needs is a check-off list for "twelve easy steps to perfect sight-reading." Choral musicians would sing praises in beautiful harmony in response to such a wonderful innovation! Oh what joy one could experience if the agony of teaching notes might be easily resolved.

There are, actually, several good sight-reading instruction programs available. (One very popular new one is *Successful Sight-Singing* by Nancy Telfer, published by the Neil A. Kjos Music Company.) It is not the intention of this chapter, however, to evaluate the different sight-reading methods but rather to provide a few supplementary ideas to assist in the use of programs already available.

Music sight-reading is not a philosophical concept which demands clinical discussion. It is a physical-mental technical skill and it can only be learned by some form of habit training. A sight-reading approach cannot be successful if development of new habits is not demanded and if constant checks on successful goal attainment are not an integral part of the total program. As in a typical speed-reading course, clearly perceived levels of attainable proficiency must be dictated. The few minutes spent on training the sight-reading skills should be the most intense, concentrated, and fast-paced part of the rehearsal, yet punctuated with laughter and light-heartedness.

Since written music is the subject to be sight-read and comprehended, then it is music notation, and, in the case of choral music, music and words, which need concentrated attention throughout the training process. All training procedures should be immediately related to "real" music. Sight-reading expertise is gained through the constant practical application of reading music at sight.

Music notation becomes the object of instruction, and therefore, the practical aspects of the present system of musical symbols must be thoroughly examined and explained. Ensemble members who do not know the important intricacies of music notation should be required to first memorize the basics of key structure, notes, and rhythm and then use this knowledge to understand more complicated constructions. Memorization soon contributes to workable habits if the memory is forced to recall quickly and often.

It is helpful to bring the music keyboard into the training procedure when teaching sight-reading. Somehow, when one looks at the note and key relationships on the keyboard, the way is eased toward a quicker vocal association. Plastic octave keyboards work well if a piano is not available.

Good rehearsal habits should be observed when sight-reading. For example:

1. When one is working with a particularly distraught section, the other ensemble sections should be encouraged to sing their own parts quietly, just as when preparing the materials for performance. The quiet sounds from other sections will help the singers of the uncertain section to find their place in the overall harmonic sound, as an adjunct to learning the individual line that is being played for them. Rehearsal time will be saved and there is less temptation for other singers to talk to each other.
2. "Forte" and "piano" symbols should be observed as well as "crescendo" and "decrescendo" signs.
3. Sight-reading voices should not be allowed to show signs of stress. Rather, a healthy vocal tone should be required.

A workable knowledge of music sight-reading builds the confidence needed to approach new musical challenges. Solid, fast growth periods in an ensemble rely on securely learned sight-reading skills. Rehearsals become more relaxed and considerably more rewarding as a result of excellence in sight-reading ability.

CHAPTER

XIII

THE CHURCH CHOIR: ATYPICAL SOLUTIONS
FOR TYPICAL PROBLEMS

If one were to use the terms "wobbly soprano," "nicotine tenor," "bull-frog bass," or "hooty alto," many a church choir director would wince with understanding. When this earthly life no longer exists, surely the church choir director and the church organist (no matter how scandalous the earthly life) will have a special quiet corner for recuperation.

However, if the church choir is typical, no more wonderful personalities can be found anywhere, and quite often life-long friendships develop as a result of church choir associations. Frustration sets in, however, when a church organist-choir director attempts to meet the challenge of a wide variety of voice training versus no training, age maturity versus no maturity, and varying musical tastes.

Most churches feel rather strongly about being "theologically correct," and music is expected to support such correctness. This concept challenges the choral conductor who wishes to place emphasis on literature of quality from the different historical eras while enhancing worship without sacrificing high performance standards. Certainly the conductor wishes to have final control with music selections. Many elements other than "theological correctness" must be considered in the choice of literature: music, lead time to prepare, etc. Battles over the choice of music can be stimulating if one keeps a good sense of humor and is not in a hurry for results.

The Wobbly Soprano
A church choir is so often characterized by that one wonderful soprano who has a wide, wide wobble in her voice. She is not necessarily an older woman. Quite often she is one who has had voice training some years ago and who has allowed an individual rehearsal regimen to assume a low priority in her life.

Generally the "wobbly" soprano does not know she has a problem, and if she does, a feeling of paranoia sets in (which makes the problem worse). Before this probably very faithful choir member is asked to use her talents in the congregation, investigate several ways of integrating voice and personality into the choral unit and subtly require great individual discipline from that singer.

If the "wobbly" soprano does not believe that the wide vibrato is the most holy way to sing the songs of praise, the choral expert can subtly suggest that the usual remedy for a wide vibrato is a relaxation of muscular tightness. The singer should be encouraged to set aside five minutes a day for some vocal exercises to help alleviate this problem.

If a singer has had voice training, muscles have been trained to act with strength upon the vocal folds and the area around the folds. As with muscular training in other parts of the body, muscle control is gained by exercise coupled with brain stimulation. The muscles, tendons, membranes, etc. surrounding the vocal mechanism, therefore, are subject to becoming flabby if the exercise habit is not nurtured. The voice reacts to this flabbiness in the form of a wide vibrato.

Some of the better remedies for the singer who wishes to return some of the muscular strength is to work on a relaxed "mm" to an "ee" or "ay" vowel and back to the "mm" and then to the "oo" vowel on a pitch that is very easy but moderately high (Illustration 17).

Illustration 17

mm ———— ee ———— ay ———— mm ———— oo

Exercises using these vowel sounds can be used even when practicing anthems. Such an approach often keeps the larger muscles from performing heavy duty work and keeps those muscles relaxed for the heavy work later required.

To try a tense, restrictive approach to calming the wide vibrato will just make the situation worse. We cannot stop the aging process, but we can keep trying to tone up the physical properties around the vocal cage.

Although a conscious speeding up of a wide vibrato by the soprano will work with a few problematic soprano choristers, with most sopranos such a treatment will cause tensions creating a lack of vibrato evenness. When a singer senses that the voice is out-of-control because of uneven vibrato, a new problem is created which is greater than the original. It is suggested that if an approach of directed vibrato speed-up is dictated and the effect is not immediate, the exercise should be abandoned.

Balance and Blend

Church choir directors often feel compelled, for political reasons, to allow members of the choir who have been sitting together enjoying friendly visits for many years to remain together. We are also influenced by tradition which states that the sopranos and altos must sit in the front row with tenors and basses behind the lines of women. This is not necessarily the best arrangement for optimum sound.

When the ear is used as a critical measurement tool, the musical director finds that, as a result of a variety of vocal sounds created by different training backgrounds and age, very little is happening as far as blend and balance are concerned when the singers are in a usual bloc formation. We can either pass the problem off as just the typical church choir scene or we can find a workable system to help gain a semblance of balance and blend.

I would like to offer a few suggestions to attain a better balance and a more interesting blend. These suggestions concerning church choir blend are aimed toward the smaller ensemble numbering from 12 to 40.

Basses and Sopranos

Among the number of singers in a typical church choir, no matter how small, will be the throaty "bull-frog bass" who sings slightly flat but who has a nice thick color to his voice. This ensemble member is a prime candidate for a "filter" voice, and could very well be considered early in the blend game for a front row position. To even think of placing an out-of-tune bass in the front row produces chills up and down a conductor's spine, but this heavy, low-format placement can filter out some of the less-desirable soprano quality if the sopranos are placed behind the "bull-frog" bass. This bass may, as a result, begin to listen more carefully to himself and sing more in tune.

Quite often when a "wobbly" soprano is placed between two lyric soprano qualities and arranged in back of a throaty bass surrounded by other basses of varying qualities (Illustration 18), the wide vibrato of the soprano is modified and the flatness of the bass is partially corrected by the soprano quality piercing both the ear and sound profile of the bass in question.

Illustration 18

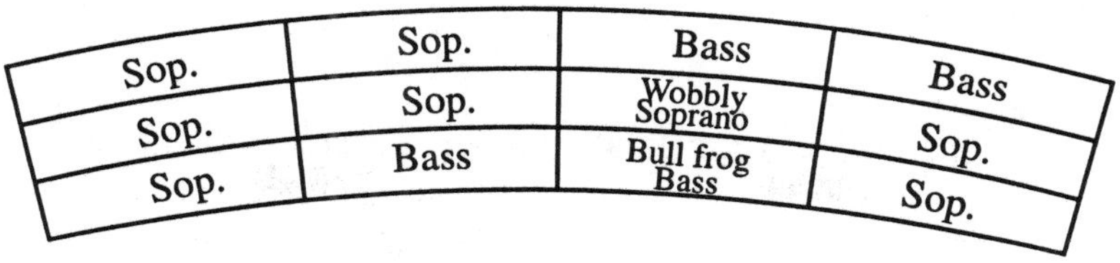

Sop.	Sop.	Bass	Bass
Sop.	Sop.	Wobbly Soprano	Sop.
Sop.	Bass	Bull frog Bass	Sop.

For an overall blend, if the ensemble has two or three clear, in-tune sopranos, these sopranos should make up the first short row, while the second row of singers might include most of the basses, with the third row containing the problem soprano voice qualities (Illustration 19). When using this placement, the basses are used as the filtering element for the third row and as a modifying quality for the first row.

Illustration 19

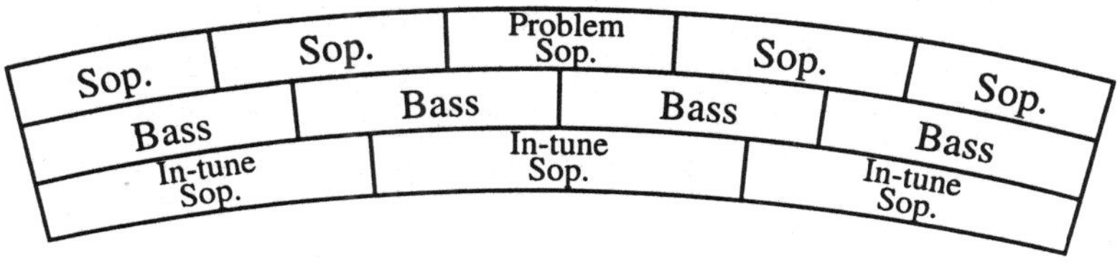

Sop.	Sop.	Problem Sop.	Sop.	Sop.
Bass	Bass	Bass	Bass	
In-tune Sop.		In-tune Sop.		In-tune Sop.

It certainly is no easy task to convince a church ensemble to experiment with such an arrangement. Quite often, however, the results in better blend are rather striking and satisfying to singer, conductor, and congregation alike. To satisfy curiosity, just explain that you are trying to solve some acoustical problems. More detailed explanations might be tendered outside of rehearsal time in response to questions asked.

Altos and Tenors

Now, to the other side of the choir with the "hooty" alto and the "nicotine" tenor. The altos are the "filters" for this side of the choral ensemble. They are not, however, as effective as the basses at filtering—especially if most of the altos sing with a back-of-the-head "hoot" rather than a forward quality which might better carry the tone.

The secret to promoting blend and balance between the altos and the tenors is to place the tenor voice (which has somewhat of a cutting edge to its quality) behind the dull sound of the "hooty" alto (Illustration 20). If this dull alto sound is framed by the modified or lighter alto voices (sopranos who sing the alto part due to lack of real altos) and the tenor's quality is drilling through the modified alto voices, quite often the full mezzo quality of the real (but "hooty") alto will permeate the alto section, giving a pleasing quality of overall alto sound.

Illustration 20

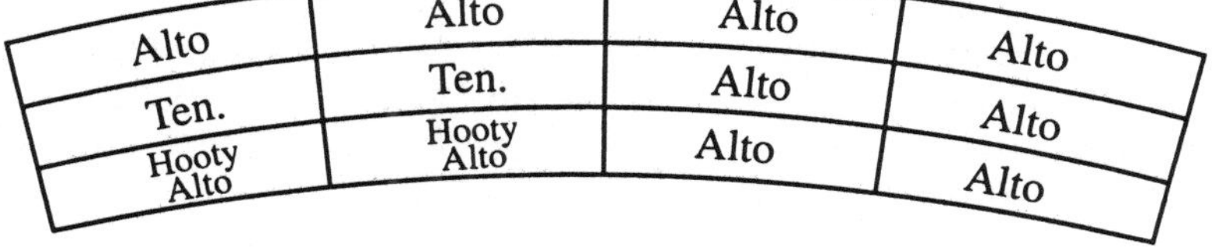

Alto	Alto	Alto	Alto
Ten.	Ten.	Alto	Alto
Hooty Alto	Hooty Alto	Alto	Alto

In the meantime, the tenor quality of sound may be less than satisfying and probably not in true pitch. Such a situation is difficult to handle, for the church choir often has not more than two or three tenors in attendance. A blend through movement of personnel, therefore, is difficult to achieve.

If the tenors are middle-age added problems are quickly evident. The tenor ensemble member may have been smoking for thirty years which means an accumulation of tar on the vocal folds. That situation translates into a flatness in pitch caused by slower fold vibrations per second. To solve this problem the nicotine tenor has to be made aware of the problem to the extent that he will always think of producing a tone higher than that to which he is accustomed. (Other singers may have problems due to smoking, but their voices don't seem to be as strongly affected as those of tenors.)

Another common problem among middle-age tenors is a rather metallic quality that creeps into the tenor voice over the years. Such a metallic quality is usually the result of losing the ability for the head voice to carry the projected sound. (Quite often the problem is a result of using a professional-sounding chest speaking voice in his profession.) The tenor who has this problem has to be prodded again and again during rehearsal to lighten the quality and allow the "ping" to reappear in the vocal placement.

Of course, most church choirs can claim at least one wonderful high baritone who must sing tenor to balance out the section. The only advice I have to offer for such an important contributor to the church choir is to allow the performer to use falsetto when the tessitura is high and to implore the baritone not to strain in voice production.

The quality of sound coming from the usual interesting array of tenor vocal production can, to a certain extent, be manipulated by placing (through experimentation) the alto voices in front of the tenor cones of sound. Quite often a mezzo quality from the alto section will improve the metallic tenor quality and a bright alto sound will help the intonation of the tenor who is flat in pitch. If the tenors are independent enough when it comes to singing the prescribed parts, placing an alto between two tenors can greatly help the general blend of the alto and tenor sections.

The typical church choir's penchant for having fun during a rehearsal, and the easy repartee of the choir members often eases the trauma of new seating in the choir loft. One can only hope that those choir members who love to joke and "loosen up" the choir during rehearsals (and, dare say, church services) will do their "thing" while seating arrangements are being changed.

Coping With the Divided Chancel

This acoustical problem is all too often confronted by the church choir director. If the contemporary architects who have designed modern versions of the divided chancel had remained faithful to the acoustical properties of the old European cathedrals, few blending problems would exist when placing the choir in a face-to-face position. The attractiveness of design and certain liturgical aims, however, seem to have taken precedence over acoustical needs when designing the modern sanctuary. As a result church choirs have to suffer the consequences of stifled voice production and poor sectional balance.

After having served several churches with divided chancel construction, I suggest discarding all ideas of sectional rows and discriminately choose the best-trained and most pleasant voices for primary placement. Each row can be considered a performing module with the finest performers placed in the outside positions and those members with lesser abilities graduated toward the end of the row farthest from the congregation (Illustration 21). If a four-part blend is desired, each row must be populated by a different part and, once again, with the strong singers toward the outside of the row. Usually, very little attention needs to be placed on how individual voices blend, for the dull acoustics have a way of modifying the sound spectrum.

Illustration 21

+ = Strong voice   - = Weak voice

B-	S-
B-	S-
B	S
B+	S+

A-	A-
A	A-
A	T
A+	A+

———————————————— Congregation ————————————————

One positive note concerning the contemporary design of split chancels is that a choir can accommodate quite an imbalance between sections without destroying overall tonal balance because the primary placement carries the weight of performance and sets the overall blend. Since the vocal instrument is basically directional, perhaps the choir can be turned at an angle facing the congregation to help the overall blending and carrying power.

Another alternative is to have the choir move for the anthem to a regular choir position in the chancel or on the stairs—if approved by church decision makers.

Literature for the Church Choir

It is too bad that so much church choral music has been relegated to the "show choir" type of literature, and that the choir feels the necessity either to get the congregation dancing in the aisles or to bring a tear to each listener's eye. The bad news concerning this trend is that much of the literature of the past is not considered emotionally-correct and, as such, not theologically stimulating. This literature is, therefore, placed in storage. The good news is that interesting and well-written music is being offered by some of our contemporary composers who are not bowing to the "cutesy tune" approach.

A musician who is a part of the church music community has to develop a certain stubbornness when dealing with ministers, committees, and individual power figures within the church. The perception held by too many ministers that music is merely mood preparation of the congregation for the sermon is certainly a high form of vanity. The idea that the anthem and the sermon should contain a common theme is a probable flight of fancy, for good anthems covering every sermon topic are not always available or musically practical. If sermon topics are available two or three months in advance, anthems can be sought that will blend with or reinforce those topics. A long lead time is necessary, of course, for procurement and rehearsal of suitable materials.

It may be suggested that the responsibility when selecting music for church is to provide the congregation with positive theological reinforcement. The presentation of the choral literature should be of the highest standard of high-quality performance. It must be pointed out that the offering of musical dregs on the altar to whatever Deity one worships just does not make sense, especially if the sermon is of the highest form. Music can stand on its own as an art form in the typical church service.

There may always be disagreement as to the place music should hold in the worship service, but the fascinating challenge to the music director is to set ever higher and more stimulating standards without being dismissed from the position of music director.

CHAPTER XIV

SOME MISCELLANEOUS "WHYS"

Musicals, Opera, and Pop Groups

Why is it not always good to present musicals in the spring?
If only choir members are allowed to participate in such a project, and if the choral conductor is in charge of the vocal part of the event, the musical or opera can be one of the finest voice-training clinics imaginable. Those who have individual roles are required to use their vocal abilities to the fullest extent to be heard, but, at the same time, learn the physical limits in order to preserve stamina.

The "stars" must be educated to move physically while using both personality and voice. This development of skills is excellent training for choral ensemble singing. Voice styling as heard on Broadway does not need to be a part of a school production—just role stylization.

The musical or opera probably should be considered for the first six weeks of the new performance season (perhaps October). As a result, the individual voices will be opened nicely in preparation for excellence in other ensemble work to be performed during the concert year.

Why do we allow "pop" groups to get by without fully using individual vocal capabilities?
Microphones and expensive amplifiers do not a vocal mechanism make! Why do we keep hearing "pop" groups who use a thin, unsupported, colorless vocal tone and who try to "look cute" to cover up anemic vocal sounds, or who, conversely, sing with destructive strident voices to try to overwhelm the microphone with a sledgehammer approach?

There are examples of beautifully blended well-trained voices, original music, and fine choreography on many university campuses. It has been my experience that high school voices can be (and should be) trained to use their full vocal abilities just as many universities groups are trained to do. The only difference will be in the maturity of vocal power: this problem can be partially solved by using "broad spectrum" microphones some distance from the singers.

If educational motives are of high priority, a "cutesy" non-vocal approach to the performance of musicals cannot be considered a worthwhile addition to any music program. If excellence in vocal training is a high priority, the "pop" choir will be able to enhance the total music program.

Tempo
Why do so many in this profession have the idea that a faster tempo is a panacea for most musical ills?
Unless the tempo is too slow in the first place, a faster tempo usually complicates any problem rather than offering a solution. To help determine the proper tempo try the following:
1. Use a dramatically slower tempo, then perform up to tempo. The tempo requested by the composer or editor might then seem comfortable.
2. Try changing keys rather than tempo—go to keys both higher and lower than the original, then back to the indicated key.

3. Change tempos erratically (slow to fast to medium, etc.) then revert back to the original strict tempo.
4. At the indicated tempo, use vowels and consonants in a nonsensical, unrelated way instead of the text, then sing through with text.
5. Sing the composition on the vowel "ay," then with the printed text.

There are also basic solutions as a substitute for changing the tempo. The list is not all that lengthy, but variations are numerous and open to the conductor's creativity. A list of some possible ways to rectify a problem without resorting to a faster tempo includes:
1. correct posture
2. efficient breathing
3. beautiful vowel color
4. musical consonants
5. muscular discipline

In this business a solution for one problem may very well not transfer from one ensemble to the next. Use of these methods and their variations is vital to excellence in choral performance.

Rhythm
Why do some choral conductors conduct individual rhythms rather than time signatures?
Ensemble singers surely do not have an average mental capability below that of instrumentalists that makes them incapable of understanding rhythmic concepts. (Perhaps the typical vocal ensemble member is brighter than the average person and subsequently makes the conductor do all the work!)

Choral conductors should demand counting ability and musical accountability from the performer. Singers will observe musical markings if their excuses for not being observant are not accepted. Exercises should be devised to thoroughly teach the choral musician difficult rhythms such as three against two or four against three when that is necessary for the music being performed. The average singer is bright enough to quickly react to basic musicianship and demands for individual initiative.

Rewards of Excellence
Why is singing in a fine choral ensemble often so rewarding?
Many have pondered this question for years, and still have not reached an acceptable answer. At this stage in my life I no longer want an answer—just a continuation of the satisfaction of a high aesthetic fulfillment.

May we, conductors and singers, often experience the excitement and emotional rewards which result from making choral music come alive.

CHAPTER

The Art of Choral Accompanying
by Marie Johnson

Occasionally choral accompanying is referred to as merely "pounding out the notes." No knowledgeable keyboard artist would make such a statement! Conductors always hope for accompanists who take a more musical approach to their responsibilities. `

The choral accompanist should use the same fine tone, phrasing, and general musical approach that is used in a solo recital. The only difference is that it is the conductor who determines the fine points of interpretation and controls the tempo. The accompanist should be able to ascertain these points by careful attention to the conductor's movements as well as to spoken instructions.

Accompanying the Choral Rehearsal

Most choirs will need a certain amount of help from the accompanist while learning a new composition. Unless the accompanist is an extremely good sight-reader, he or she will need study and practice time before the rehearsal. The accompanist will then be prepared to play single lines, full vocal score, or printed accompaniment as needed and always in a musical manner. It is imperative that the conductor give the scores to the accompanist well in advance if the accompanist is not a good sight reader. It is unfortunate if the accompanist is just learning the music along with the choir, thereby holding back rehearsal progress.

Playing open score is not easy for many accompanists. If there are several extra parts or the rhythm is especially difficult, there is no reason why one cannot lightly pencil in the alto with the soprano and the tenor with the bass or some variation of this "crutch."

When playing single parts, there is seldom a need to "pound." If the singers are on the correct notes, they don't need to hear the keyboard. If they are singing wrong notes, they will hear the right ones because they are "different." It is often helpful to play the line very softly an octave higher (at the same time as playing as written). On the organ this can be accomplished by adding a four-foot stop.

When playing parts, it is better for organists to use flute stops rather than string stops (which blend too readily with the voice). Principal stops are also good. Avoid the temptation to throw on full organ because the singers need to be able to hear themselves.

If, during the early stages of learning new music, the accompanist plays slightly ahead of the beat, the singers will find it helpful while honing their sight-reading skills. Do not, however, get in the habit of doing this all of the time!

As the singers become more comfortable with the parts, the accompanist should "back away"—first by playing very softly and then by stopping the playing of the parts. The accompanist's attention should never leave the music being sung as some parts may falter and need some help from the keyboard. The rehearsal will progress more rapidly if the accompanist is ready to "jump in" whenever needed rather than making it necessary for the conductor to stop the whole choir and go back to work out the difficult passage. The accompanist should check with the conductor before using this procedure, however, as some conductors like to have the singers "struggle" just a bit so that they will keep their attention on the music.

Remember that all of this will be accomplished with musical tone, phrasing, and dynamics. Some singers tend to copy what they are hearing from the piano. The fewer bad habits that must be remedied by the conductor the faster the rehearsal will move along.

Dealing With Orchestral Reductions

When working with an accompaniment that is a keyboard reduction of a full orchestral score, the accompanist may find it impossible to reach all of the notes indicated. It is quite acceptable to do some editing of one's own and omit some notes. It's helpful to consult a full score to discover the original instrumental lines if piano accompaniment is to be used in performance.

If there is a second accompanist who can assist, part of the lines of the accompaniment may be played by that person. In this case it is a good idea to have a look at the full orchestral score and consider including some musical lines that were omitted in order to design the accompaniment to fit the capability of four hands on the keyboard. Try to divide the accompaniment between the two players so that single instrumental lines are carried through by the same player. For example, do not divide a particular clarinet line between the two players as this will disturb the phrasing of that line.

The Performance

When accompanying on a grand piano, it should be remembered that the lid should not be left closed. It should be raised at least a bit to avoid the muffled tone otherwise produced. If there is no "short stick" on the piano, the lid can be raised slightly by inserting a book for the lid to rest on.

Some accompanists think that the lid should be down so that they can play softly enough. They wouldn't play a recital that way, of course, or expect the singer to place a hand over the mouth to produce a pianissimo sound! Nor does a trumpet player use the mute for the sole purpose of producing a soft sound (rather, a certain tone quality).

Any accomplished pianist can produce a pianissimo when needed. It is a bit more difficult to come up with a fortissimo to match that of a "healthy" choral organization. A choir is probably capable of greater dynamic contrasts than any single singer or instrument. The only times when the piano lid should remain closed are when the pianist is not very accomplished or the piano tone is impossibly harsh.

When playing an organ accompaniment, the organist should take advantage of the full range of stops available to properly support and complement the choir and the repertoire (contrary to certain limitations for rehearsal). If the written accompaniment is an orchestral reduction, get a copy of the full score to discover the original instrumentation and consider organ registration which approximates the sound of the orchestra.

At the "dress rehearsal" it is helpful to have someone out in the auditorium to listen for proper balance between accompaniment and choir. Acoustics can be deceiving. This fact is especially true with organ accompaniment. The listener should indicate problems of loud and soft, then allow the accompanist to make the correction (i.e. don't tell the organist which stops to use).

When the choir is singing *a cappella*, the accompanist, after giving pitches in a musical manner, should listen intently to what the choir is producing—not looking at the audience or getting the next piece ready!

The accompanist needs to use the eyes and ears as well as the fingers, to play with the vowels—not the beginning consonants, listen carefully for dynamics in order to keep proper balance between choir and accompaniment, and to watch the conductor for changes in tempo and interpretation that may be a bit different from those used in rehearsal.

The choral accompanist's creed should be: Be Prepared, Be Musical, Be Responsive.